Reasons to Roast

To Kathy,
Happy Roasting,
Enjoy,
Sandra Dramard

Reasons to Roast

More Than 100 Simple and Intensely Flavorful Recipes

G E O R G I A   C H A N   D O W N A R D
A N D   E V I E   R I G H T E R

I L L U S T R A T I O N S   B Y   D O R O T H Y   R E I N H A R D T

A Chapters Book

HOUGHTON MIFFLIN COMPANY
BOSTON   NEW YORK
1997

Library of Congress Cataloging-in-Publication Data

Downard, Georgia
    Reasons to roast: more than 100 simple and intensely flavorful recipes /
by Georgia Chan Downard, Evie Righter; illustrated by Dorothy Reinhardt.
        p.   cm.
Includes index.
ISBN 1-57630-061-7 (pbk.)
1. Roasting (Cookery). I. Righter, Evie. II. Title.
TX690.D69   1997
641.7'1—dc21   97-13760

Printed in Canada
00 10 9 8 7 6 5 4 3 2 1

Cover illustration by Dorothy Reinhardt
Designed by Susan McClellan

To Auntie Noni, with love
—*G.C.D.*

To David, Sam and Henry,
for the untold pleasure of your company
and for the fun we have in seeing my projects
through to the end
—*E.R.*

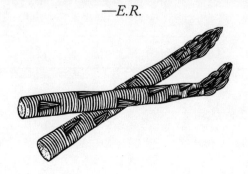

Acknowledgments

Our heartfelt thanks to Tina Sharpe, for her dedication, creativeness and, above all, friendship. We would also like to thank Madeleine Morel, our agent, for her timing and perceptiveness, and our editor, Rux Martin, whose steadfast determination and insight helped shape this book.

$\mathcal{C}$ontents

When company descends, don't panic. Make it easy on yourself and slip a pan of *Asian Honey-Roasted Peanuts* into the oven, while you concentrate on preparing the rest of the dinner. Or set out a bowl of *Roasted Tortilla Chips* with *Roasted Corn Salsa,* and enjoy your own party. For a more elaborate first course, serve *Indonesian Roasted Pork Cubes with Peanut Dipping Sauce* or *Oysters Casino,* topped with crisp bits of bacon and shallots.

Chapter II . . . Soups . . . 59

For richness of flavor without adding cream, roast ingredients before adding them to the soup pot. Try *Roasted Pumpkin Soup* or velvety *Roasted Sweet Potato and White Bean Chowder with Sage* and see for yourself. In the winter, start your meal with *Roasted Onion and Leek Soup* topped with crisp *Gruyère and Parmesan Croûtes*; or enjoy this soup as a simple supper. For summer, *Chilled Roasted Red Pepper Soup with Feta and Dill* sings with flavor.

Chapter III . . . Shellfish and Fish . . . 81

For a special event, nothing surpasses fish and shellfish. Recipes include *Roasted Lobster with Tomato and Basil Essence, Sea Scallops Roasted in Bacon* and *Roasted Shrimp in Lemony Garlic Butter*. Or bring out a whole *Roasted Sea Bass with Bread Stuffing*. Most of these recipes are ready in minutes. Set your timer!

Chapter IV . . . Poultry . . . 109

Something for everyone: from an utterly simple and dependable *Roasted Lemon Chicken* to a down-to-earth oven-cooked *Barbecued Chicken* to a mouthwatering *Maple-Glazed Roasted Duckling with McIntosh Apples*. And for the centerpiece of the holiday table, a resplendent *Roasted Turkey with Herbed Sausage and Pecan Stuffing*, served with *Roasted Pearl Onion and Raisin Compote*.

Chapter V . . . Meat . . . 143

Roasted Peppered Tenderloin of Beef with Port Wine Sauce, Roasted Veal Chops with Sage, Roasted Butterflied Leg of Lamb with English Mint Sauce—these are just a few of the spectacular possibilities. And for carefree weeknight suppers, *Pork Sausages Roasted with Onions and Apples* or *Brown-Sugar-and-Soy-Marinated Roast Pork Tenderloin*.

Chapter VI . . . Vegetables . . . 171

Roasting is as convenient as boiling but yields twice the taste, as flavorful as grilling, with half the hassle. You'll find easy recipes for all seasons, from *Roasted Asparagus with Parmesan* for spring to a summery *Corn on the Cob Roasted with Jalapeño-and-Cilantro Butter* to *Slow-Roasted Onions* and *Roasted Broccoli with Lemon Garlic Butter and Toasted Pine Nuts* for fall and winter.

Chapter VII . . . Salads . . . 201

With innovative combinations and focused flavors, these salads are stars in their own right. From *Roasted Portobello Mushroom and Arugula Salad* to *Roasted Red Pepper and Fennel Salad with Cannellini Beans* to *Peppered Tuna Salad Niçoise*, many can be served as first or main courses.

Chapter VIII . . . Desserts . . . 223

The preparations are easy, the cooking times short, the eating sweet. Choose from a dozen fast fruit selections, such as *Roasted Pineapple* and *Roasted Bananas with Caramel Sauce.* You'll also find desserts that are quicker than cobblers and crisps but just as luscious, like *Peach Bruschetta.* And *Roasted Brioche and Chocolate Sandwiches* make a spontaneous indulgence for any occasion, including breakfast.

Index . . . 245

Introduction

$\mathcal{R}$*easons to Roast* was born out of a love of good food. When we each ticked off our favorite dishes, then compared notes, we found that our lists included many of the same items: roast chicken—the burnished and juicy kind—standing rib roast, served with Yorkshire pudding that looked like the surface of the moon but tasted heavenly; a turkey that would start roasting early Thanksgiving morning for the midafternoon feast; garlicky roasted new potatoes, crispy on the outside, soft and sweet within and totally irresistible.

Roasting not only produces incomparable results but also suits the demands of our lifestyles, as it did for our mothers. When we roast, dinner can be on the table without any fuss, and we can still handle the thousand other things that seem to pop up at the same time at the end of our busy workdays. Once the dish is in the oven, it requires little else, save, perhaps, occasional basting. The oven—not the cook—does the work. The number of times each of us has put a chicken in to roast for a simple but special dinner is irrefutable proof of the method's ease.

We began to experiment. Instead of whole chicken, we tried roasting just the legs and wings, with even faster results. We discovered that roasting fish and shellfish is quicker still. Vegetables like green beans and fennel tasted every bit as good as our favorite potatoes when roasted. It did not take us long to agree that roasting a butternut squash before pureeing it for a soup or roasting beets for an endive salad was well worth the little amount of extra effort. Nuts mixed with a variety of seasonings and roasted made great gifts or instant snacks before dinner. Roasted garlic became ineffably sweet, perfect for adding to dips or spreading on toasted bread. Pineapples, apples and peaches took on a new dimension in the oven.

Meat that has been roasted develops a crisp brown crust, while the interior remains juicy. For that reason, sauces are usually unnecessary. Roasted fish and shellfish is firm outside, never mushy, with incomparable moistness within. Mushrooms become meatier, squash sweeter and roasted green vegetables like asparagus and beans are standouts, their taste undiluted by cooking water. And there is another dividend of roasting: few calories, little fat.

THOUGH THE USES WE WERE PUTTING IT TO WERE NEW, roasting is in fact the world's oldest cooking method, dating to prehistoric times, when a hunk of meat was stuck on a pointed stick and cooked over an open fire. At some point—exactly when is not certain—spit-roasting moved inside to the hearth. Starting at least as far back as the Middle Ages in Europe and the 1700s in North America, meat was roasted in the fireplace. Then in the mid-1800s, the flame gave way to the oven, and since that time, roasting has meant cooking in dry heat, uncovered, without added liquid.

Despite the simplicity of roasting, debates on the best way to do it are practically as old as the method itself. You can roast at high heat for a short time, at a moderate temperature for a longer time, or at an initial high heat and then at a lower temperature for the remainder of the time. Because the cooking method should be dictated by the food itself, we cannot categorically favor one style of roasting over another. For us, a dandy dish that tastes good, not the endorsement of one method over another, is the goal. But whether you are making Roasted Lemon Chicken, Prime Rib of Beef with Shiitake Mushroom Sauce or Roasted Bing Cherries, some guiding principles should be kept in mind for best results.

Capitalizing on the inherently healthful nature of roasting, we have kept the fat to a minimum. And, so that getting a meal on the table can be as effortless for you as it has been for us, we have included preparation and cooking times for each recipe.

General Pointers on Roasting

❖ Know your oven. Be sure its thermostat is calibrated accurately. If in doubt, before roasting anything, test it yourself with a mercury oven thermometer. We've found that the more often an oven is used on high heat, the more often it will need to be recalibrated.

❖ While smoke was not a factor for us, it has been known to occur when roasting. Ideally, your stove has a hood and well-working exhaust fan. If it does not, crack the kitchen window when roasting at high temperatures. Better yet, if you're able, cross-ventilate.

❖ If you do not own an instant-read thermometer for testing meats and poultry, we recommend that you purchase one. The cooking times in the following recipes reflect our own tastes: You may want to adjust the times to suit your own preferences, and there is nothing like a thermometer to eliminate the guess factor. Look for instant-read thermometers in specialty cookware stores and in the equipment section of better-stocked supermarkets.

❖ As to cookware for roasting, we recommend heavy-gauge metal pans with a stainless steel wash. Enameled cast-iron and enameled steel are both good heat conveyors too. At all costs, avoid lightweight roasting pans, as they can warp from the heat of a high oven. Low-sided pans are generally preferable, because they allow liquids to evaporate quickly so foods brown rather than steam. To roast a Thanksgiving turkey, however, we like to use the traditional high-sided pan, which helps prevent the basting juices from spattering all over the oven.

Handles on a roasting pan are an important feature. More often than not a roast is heavy, and taking it in and out of the hot oven is something of a challenge. Handles make the job a lot easier and safer. So do truly heat-resistant oven mitts . . . for both hands.

❖ A roasting rack is not necessary unless stipulated—which it generally is for poultry. You want the skin on the bottom of the bird to roast, not cook in the pan juices; a rack facilitates that.

About the Recipes

❖ Allow at least 20 minutes to preheat the oven.

❖ Unless the recipe indicates otherwise, roast on the middle rack of the oven, where temperatures are more even.

❖ Remember that foods roasted at high temperatures, especially meat and poultry, will continue to cook after being removed from the oven. Be careful not to overcook.

❖ A digital kitchen timer is the most accurate kind. Stove clocks may or may not be trustworthy; our experience is that they are not.

❖ Let cooked meat and poultry stand, tented loosely with foil to keep the heat in, for 10 to 15 minutes so the juices settle back into the meat.

❖ Learn to trust your own judgment. If something smells as if it is overcooking, chances are it is. Your nose is a very reliable guide!

*M*enus

COME FOR DRINKS AND GOOD FOOD

HERE IS A VERY DOABLE MENU that can be prepared in advance. It features nonfilling finger food, the kind that most people find irresistible. In fact, we don't even need the excuse of a party to prepare these kinds of dishes. At any given time, we have two or three stored in our pantry or refrigerator. The potato skins are positively addictive: Prepare a double batch, and be sure to keep your family out of the kitchen while you're cooking, or you'll have to make them all over again.

❖

Roasted Almonds with Golden Raisins   *(page 28)*

Roasted Parmesan Popcorn   *(page 32)*

Roasted Eggplant and Tahini Dip   *(page 36)*

Roasted Sesame Pita Chips   *(page 33)*

Roasted Garlic and Cream Cheese Dip served with crudités   *(page 40)*

Roasted Potato Skins with Monterey Jack Cheese and Chipotle Chiles   *(page 44)*

❖

THE FLAVORS OF GREECE

SERVE THIS LIGHT GREEK-INSPIRED MENU on a summer evening on the patio or terrace. The soup must be prepared in advance, which makes its timing straightforward. Prepare the plums ahead of time as well. The snapper and zucchini can be cooked at the same time: The snapper roasts at 450°F for 25 minutes, the zucchini for 15 minutes. And who's to know how steamy the kitchen is if you are dining outdoors?

Have a nice bottle of Italian Tocai or American Chardonnay to drink with the snapper and, depending upon how daring you feel, some retsina, too, to put you in the Mediterranean mood.

❖

Chilled Roasted Red Pepper Soup with Feta and Dill *(page 78)*

Roasted Red Snapper Greek Style *(page 100)*

Roasted Zucchini with Red Onion *(page 199)*

Roasted Prune Plums with Almond Topping *(page 232)*

❖

A THANKSGIVING DINNER

THIS IS THE KIND OF MENU our mothers served year after year . . . and no child of theirs has been able to improve upon it. There are no frills in these dishes, but the flavors, textures and colors are fabulous. Feel free to add a pie or vanilla ice cream for dessert too. We also serve a bowl of whipped potatoes for the turkey gravy.

As to a game plan for making the dinner, the nuts, soup and compote can all be done several days in advance. Make the stuffing the day before Thanksgiving and keep it covered in the refrigerator. On Thanksgiving Day, stuff and roast the turkey and while it rests, roast the sugar snap peas or the green beans, which leaves only the pears: Put them in the oven during dinner. Alternatively, make the pears and sauce in advance too, then reheat them in the turned-off but still-warm oven while you dine.

❖

Roasted Nuts with Sugar and Spice   *(page 29)*

Roasted Pumpkin Soup with Gruyère and Parmesan Croûtes   *(page 70)*

Roasted Turkey Breast with Hazelnut and Wild Rice Stuffing   *(page 134)*

or

Roasted Turkey with Herbed Sausage and Pecan Stuffing   *(page 137)*

Roasted Pearl Onion and Raisin Compote   *(page 140)*

Roasted Sugar Snap Peas   *(page 194)*

or

Roasted Green Beans   *(page 184)*

Roasted Pears with Almond-Flavored Custard Sauce   *(page 238)*

❖

AN ANNIVERSARY DINNER

NOTHING ABOUT THIS CELEBRATORY MENU is complicated, including its timing. All the components for the salad can be prepared in advance; wait to dress it until just before serving. Plan to roast the tenderloin about 1 hour before you intend to sit down. While it roasts, enjoy your salads. Remove the beef at the appropriate moment, and while it rests, roast the asparagus and make the port wine sauce. The figs can roast while you are savoring the last of your wine. Speaking of wine, go all out with a fine Cabernet Sauvignon or Bordeaux.

❖

Roasted Portobello Mushroom and Arugula Salad *(page 206)*

Roasted Peppered Tenderloin of Beef with Port Wine Sauce *(page 152)*

Roasted Asparagus with Parmesan *(page 175)*

Roasted Figs with Mascarpone *(page 235)*

❖

A FAMILY REUNION

SIMPLE AND EASY TO DOUBLE OR TRIPLE, this menu makes hosting a family reunion—or a relaxed celebration for a wedding or after a graduation—a snap. All of the dishes can be made in advance, so you can relax and enjoy your own party. While the tomatoes are good served warm, they are also fine at room temperature. The same applies to the peaches.

The pressure, at least from the standpoint of the cook, is off! As for beverages, we recommend home-brewed beer. If there are no home-brewers in your clan, serve a selection of microbrews.

❖

Barbecued Chicken   *(page 114)*

Roasted Potato Cakes   *(page 189)*

Roasted Italian Tomatoes   *(page 195)*

Roasted Peaches with Amaretti   *(page 236)*

❖

SUPPER FOR A SNOWY NIGHT

IT MIGHT BE COLD AND BLUSTERY OUTSIDE, but it won't matter a bit when you serve a comforting menu like this. From start to finish (and that includes resting time) the chicken needs 1½ hours maximum; 1 hour and 20 minutes, to be exact. You can either make the soup—an agreeable snowy day undertaking!—during that time or prepare it in advance. The caramel sauce for the bananas can also be done ahead of time; rewarm it in a double boiler.

You will need a loaf of good bread to sop up the pan juices from the chicken. If you're snowed in, you might want to bake your favorite bread.

❖

Curried Butternut Squash Soup with Cilantro Cream   *(page 62)*

Roasted Lemon Chicken   *(page 112)*

Roasted Bananas with Caramel Sauce   *(page 230)*

❖

SNACKS AND STARTERS

Chapter I

Snacks *and* Starters

Y OU KNOW THE FEELING. Guests are coming for dinner, and you are late getting started. Everything you had planned to do from the minute you walked in the door—picking up the house, setting the table, finishing the dessert—now has to be done in triple time. Instead of panicking (or, worse, offering to take everyone out), regroup for a moment. You have a viable alternative, and it is not opening a jar or taking something out of the freezer. It is called roasting.

Especially when it comes to appetizers, nothing beats the ease of roasting. Nuts are a case in point. Once they are tossed with some well-chosen spices and placed in the oven, you are free to move on to the rest of your meal preparations. They roast virtually unattended—an important consideration when there is a lot to do but no time to do it.

There is another equally important reason to roast appetizers or finger foods: They do not rely on added fat for flavor. Eggplant, for example, can be brushed with just a light film of olive oil and roasted until it becomes exquisitely tender. It can then be combined with tahini (sesame seed paste) for a Middle Eastern dip or mashed into a "caviar" spread, seasoned with a little lemon juice, garlic and parsley. Corn can be roasted, then cut from the cob and mixed into a lively Southwest-inspired salsa. The initial step of roasting imparts nuances and subtleties of taste that boiling or steaming cannot approach.

There is no more salient example of the transformative power of roasting than what happens to garlic. The cloves soften to a spreadable consistency and turn golden. The flavor mellows and becomes ineffably sweet. Gone is the sharp, pungent bite. Thus tamed, the garlic can then be combined with cream cheese and sour cream for a savory dip for roasted or raw vegetables.

To accompany the dips, we've included a couple of recipes for tasty chips and crackers. Roasted Tortilla Chips (page 34)—corn tortillas that have been brushed with a little vegetable oil and sprinkled with Mexican seasonings—are a lower-fat, more flavorful alternative to the usual commercial fried versions. Serve them with the roasted corn salsa. Roasted Sesame Pita Chips (page 33)—pita pockets brushed with a little butter and sesame oil and sprinkled with toasted sesame seeds—go well with the Middle Eastern dips.

What follows is an eclectic collection of snacks, chips, dips, hors d'oeuvres and first courses. Some, like Roasted Shrimp and Tomato Bruschetta (page 50) and Roasted Garlic and Goat Cheese Flans (page 56), can double as light luncheon dishes when paired with a salad.

Snacks *and* Starters

Roasted Almonds *with* Golden Raisins

Makes 5½ cups
Preparation time: 5 minutes ❖ *Cooking time: 15 minutes*

I F YOU START WITH BLANCHED (skinned) almonds, this recipe is simplicity itself. And if the almonds you have on hand need blanching, there's not much to that, either: Bring a saucepan of water to a boil, add the almonds, and boil for 20 to 30 seconds; drain. While the nuts are still hot, slip them out of their skins. Pat dry or air-dry before using or storing.

3	cups (about 1 pound) blanched whole almonds		Fine-grained sea salt
1	tablespoon olive oil	1	15-ounce box (2½ cups) golden raisins

1. Preheat the oven to 425°F.

2. Spread the almonds in a single layer on a baking sheet and roast, stirring often, for 15 minutes, or until lightly golden. Drizzle the almonds with the olive oil and sprinkle with salt to taste. Let cool.

3. In a bowl, toss the almonds with the raisins. Serve as an accompaniment to drinks. Store in an airtight container.

Roasted Nuts *with* Sugar *and* Spice

Makes 2 cups

Preparation time: 15 minutes ❖ *Cooking time: 35 minutes*

A DELICIOUS AROMA fills the house while these nuts are roasting—and they taste even better than they smell. Rolling the nuts first in beaten egg whites helps the sugar-and-spice mixture adhere, making for a delightfully crispy coating. At holiday time, put them in tins and give them as gifts. Be ready to share the recipe.

2	large egg whites	¼	teaspoon ground cloves
1	teaspoon salt	2⅔	cups (¾ pound) nuts, roasted
2	cups sugar		or unroasted, such as pecans,
1	tablespoon ground cinnamon		almonds, cashews or a combination
1	teaspoon freshly grated nutmeg		

1. Preheat the oven to 325°F. Line 2 baking sheets with parchment paper.

2. In a medium bowl, whisk the egg whites with the salt until the salt dissolves. Sift together the sugar, cinnamon, nutmeg and cloves into another bowl.

3. Add the nuts to the egg whites in small batches, turning to coat them completely. With a fork, transfer each batch of nuts to the spiced sugar and toss. Place the nuts about 1 inch apart on the baking sheets and roast for 30 to 35 minutes, or until crisp. Let cool. Store in an airtight container.

Asian Honey-Roasted Peanuts

Makes 3 cups
Preparation time: 5 minutes ❖ *Cooking time: 25 minutes*

IF YOU ARE ACCUSTOMED TO STORE-BOUGHT dry-roasted peanuts from a jar, wait until you try these. They are sweet and only slightly salty, and like all peanuts—the good and the not-so-good—hard to resist. If you have any left over, coarsely crush them and sprinkle over a sesame-oil-dressed Asian noodle salad.

Purchase raw peanuts at health food stores; the fresher they are, the better.

3 tablespoons soy sauce	3 cups (about 1 pound) raw shelled peanuts
4 teaspoons peanut oil	
2 teaspoons honey	

1. Preheat the oven to 350°F. Lightly oil a baking sheet.

2. In a medium bowl, combine the soy sauce, oil and honey. Add the peanuts and toss to coat evenly. Spread the peanuts in a single layer on the baking sheet and roast, stirring occasionally, for 25 minutes, or until nicely glazed. Let cool. Store in an airtight container.

*S*low-Roasted Granola *with* Apricots *and* Almonds

Makes about 8 cups

Preparation time: 15 minutes ❖ *Cooking time: 28 minutes*

WHAT DISTINGUISHES THIS GRANOLA from others is its lightness—note the conservative amount of oil—and the simplicity of the combination. Vary the nuts and seeds as you wish, but keep the apricots; they make it special.

Granola can be served for breakfast, as a snack or as a topping for yogurt or ice cream.

4 cups old-fashioned rolled oats	½ cup honey
1 cup wheat germ	½ cup orange juice
⅔ cup raw sunflower seeds	3 tablespoons canola oil
⅔ cup sliced unblanched almonds	1 cup diced dried apricots
1½ teaspoons ground cinnamon	½ cup dark raisins

1. Preheat the oven to 325°F.

2. In a large roasting pan, combine the oats, wheat germ, sunflower seeds, almonds and cinnamon.

3. In a small saucepan, combine the honey, orange juice and oil and cook, stirring, over low heat until smooth. Pour the mixture into the roasting pan and toss until the dry ingredients are well coated. Roast, stirring frequently, for 25 minutes, or until lightly toasted. Let cool.

4. Stir in the apricots and raisins. Store in airtight containers for up to 2 months.

Roasted Parmesan Popcorn

Makes 10 cups
Preparation time: 10 minutes (does not include popping the corn)
Cooking time: 6 minutes

THERE IS A LOT TO BE SAID for making your own popcorn, especially where freshness is concerned. Reduce the amount of butter and/or spice this up with more cayenne if you wish, but use only fresh Parmesan for the best flavor. By all means, select Hungarian paprika, available at specialty food shops and some supermarkets, which is much more interesting than the usual bland red powder. We like the Szeged brand, with its beautiful old-fashioned red, white and green tin, because it has just what it says on the label: "exquisite 100% sweet delicacy."

½ cup freshly grated Parmesan	10 cups popped popcorn
2 teaspoons sweet Hungarian paprika	(¾ cup plus 2 tablespoons unpopped)
1 teaspoon garlic powder	4 tablespoons (½ stick)
Salt	unsalted butter, melted
Cayenne pepper	

1. Preheat the oven to 375°F. Lightly oil a large roasting pan.

2. In a small bowl, combine the Parmesan, paprika, garlic powder and salt and cayenne to taste. Place the popcorn in a large bowl and, using your hands, toss it with the seasoning mixture. Drizzle with the butter and stir to coat.

3. Spread the popcorn in an even layer in the roasting pan and roast it for 6 minutes, or until crisp. Transfer to a large bowl for serving.

Roasted Sesame Pita Chips

Makes 24 chips
Preparation time: 8 minutes (includes toasting the sesame seeds)
Cooking time: 8 minutes

WHEN YOU WANT A CRACKER that's a little different, remember these. They are simple to make, store well and go beautifully with dips, especially a sesame-flavored one like Roasted Eggplant and Tahini Dip (page 36). They also make a nice accompaniment to chicken salad or a bowl of soup.

It may seem like gilding the lily to toast sesame seeds before roasting them, but it really brings out their flavor. To toast, place the seeds in a small, dry skillet and cook over medium heat, stirring, until they are fragrant and an even golden brown.

3	tablespoons unsalted butter, softened		3	6-inch pita pockets, each split into 2 rounds
1	tablespoon Asian sesame oil			
½	teaspoon salt, or to taste		⅓	cup sesame seeds, toasted

1. Preheat the oven to 400°F.

2. In a small bowl, combine the butter, sesame oil and salt. Brush the cut side of each pita with the butter mixture and sprinkle with the sesame seeds.

3. Cut each pita half into 4 wedges and arrange them in a single layer on a baking sheet. Roast for 8 minutes, or until crisp. Serve warm. Store in an airtight container.

Roasted Tortilla Chips

Makes 24 chips
Preparation time: 5 minutes ❖ *Cooking time: 10 minutes*

LOOK FOR PACKAGES of white or yellow corn tortillas in the refrigerator section of supermarkets. Either will work in this recipe. The difference between these chips and many you buy in bags is that these are not fried. All you need now is the salsa, and we've got one of those too (page 38).

6	corn tortillas	1 teaspoon cumin seeds,
1	tablespoon vegetable oil	toasted and ground (see Tip)
1½	teaspoons chili powder	Salt
		Cayenne pepper

1. Preheat the oven to 450°F.

2. Lightly brush both sides of the tortillas with the oil, then cut each into 4 wedges. Arrange the wedges in a single layer on a baking sheet and roast for 5 minutes. Turn and cook for 3 to 5 minutes more, or until crisp.

3. Meanwhile, in a small bowl, combine the chili powder and cumin.

4. Place the roasted chips in a bowl, sprinkle with the spice mixture and salt and cayenne to taste, toss and serve.

❖ To toast and grind cumin seeds, place in a small, dry skillet over low heat and toast, stirring, for 3 to 5 minutes, or until fragrant. Remove from the skillet and let cool. Place the seeds in a spice grinder and grind, or crush to a powder with the back of a skillet or a rolling pin.

Roasted Eggplant "Caviar"

Makes 2 cups

Preparation time: 10 minutes ❖ *Cooking time: 35 minutes*

THERE ARE ENDLESS GREAT WAYS to prepare eggplant, many of them calling for "olive oil, as needed, for cooking." Eggplant is absorbent—spongelike, in fact. The solution is to roast it, which uses only a miserly amount of oil. It is the cooking process—not the oil—that imparts the marvelous flavor.

1	large eggplant (about 1½ pounds)	2	medium garlic cloves, minced
5	tablespoons extra-virgin olive oil		Salt and freshly ground black pepper
2	tablespoons fresh lemon juice, or more to taste	⅓	cup minced fresh parsley
			Crostini or crackers, for serving

1. Preheat the oven to 450°F. Lightly oil a baking sheet.

2. Halve the eggplant lengthwise and brush the cut sides with 2 tablespoons of the oil. Arrange the eggplant, cut side down, on the baking sheet. Roast for 30 to 35 minutes, or until the flesh is tender when tested with a fork. Remove from the baking sheet and let cool.

3. Scoop out the eggplant flesh and transfer to a medium bowl; discard the peel. Mash the eggplant with a fork. Add the remaining 3 tablespoons oil, 2 tablespoons lemon juice, the garlic and salt and pepper to taste and combine gently with the fork. Taste and add more lemon juice if needed. Chill, covered, until ready to serve.

4. Before serving, stir in the parsley. Serve with the crostini or crackers.

Roasted Eggplant *and* Tahini Dip

Makes 3 cups
Preparation time: 15 minutes ❖ Cooking time: 35 minutes

WE'D WAGER THAT MOST PEOPLE buy tahini (Middle Eastern sesame seed paste) to make hummus—the renowned dip of mashed chickpeas and garlic. But what to do with all the tahini that remains in the jar? We propose this: our version of baba ghanoush, another famous dish from the same part of the world.

Use pita triangles to scoop the dip from the bowl. While nontraditional, wedges of red bell pepper make very good scoopers too.

1 large eggplant (1½ pounds)	2 tablespoons extra-virgin olive oil
2 large garlic cloves	2 tablespoons minced fresh parsley
½ cup tahini (sesame seed paste)	Kalamata olives, for garnish
6 tablespoons fresh lemon juice, or more to taste	Lightly toasted triangles of pita bread or lavash (crisp wafer bread), for serving
¾ teaspoon salt, or more to taste	

1. Preheat the oven to 450°F. Lightly oil a baking sheet.

2. Halve the eggplant lengthwise and place it, cut side down, on the baking sheet. Roast for 30 to 35 minutes, or until the flesh is tender when tested with a fork. Remove from the baking sheet and let cool.

3. Scoop out the eggplant flesh and transfer to a food processor; discard the peel. Add the garlic, tahini, 6 tablespoons lemon juice and ¾ teaspoon salt to the food processor and process until smooth. Taste and add additional lemon juice and salt if needed.

4. Spoon the puree into a wide, shallow bowl. Drizzle with the oil and garnish with the parsley and olives. Serve with the toasted pita or lavash.

Roasted Corn Salsa

Makes 6 cups, serving 10 to 12

Preparation time: 30 minutes (includes roasting the pepper) ❖ *Cooking time: 30 minutes*

CORN THAT HAS BEEN ROASTED has a distinctly smoky flavor that marries well with some of the other favored ingredients of the cooking of the Southwest. Serve this colorful salsa as a topping for Roasted Cod Steaks (page 93), in a bowl with Roasted Tortilla Chips (page 34) for dipping, as an accompaniment to grilled poultry or as a topping for black bean salad.

This is great party food, but the recipe can be halved easily for a smaller group.

6	ears corn, silk removed but left in husks (see Tip)	1	large jalapeño pepper, seeded and minced (optional)
2	large firm but ripe tomatoes, cored and diced		Salt and freshly ground black pepper to taste
1	large red bell pepper, roasted (see opposite page), peeled, cored, seeded and diced	3	tablespoons vegetable oil
		2-3	tablespoons fresh lime juice
1	small red onion, minced	3	tablespoons minced fresh cilantro

1. Preheat the oven to 450°F.

2. Put the corn on a baking sheet and roast for 25 to 30 minutes, or until tender. When cool enough to handle, remove and discard the husks. Cut the kernels from the cobs and place in a large bowl. Add the remaining ingredients, cover and chill for at least 30 minutes before serving. Store the salsa in an airtight container in the refrigerator for up to 3 days.

❖ To remove the silk from an ear of corn in the husk, simply pull gently on the silk to free it.

TO "ROAST" BELL PEPPERS

Preparation time: 5 minutes ❖ *Cooking time: 10 minutes*

THE TECHNIQUE OF CHARRING BELL PEPPERS in order to remove their skins is actually not roasting at all, but broiling. At least that is how we do it. Whether you use direct heat from a broiler, from a grill or from a gas burner, the skins should be cooked until black and charred, at which point the flesh will have taken on a wonderful smoky note. The flavor of these peppers is superior— fresher and more intense—to that of the roasted peppers you can buy in a jar.

Red bell peppers

1. Preheat the broiler. Lightly oil a baking sheet.

2. Place the peppers on the baking sheet, leaving space in between, and broil 4 inches from the heat until charred all over, about 10 minutes; turn the peppers occasionally so they blacken evenly.

3. With tongs, transfer the peppers to a paper bag and close the bag tightly. Let the peppers steam in the bag until cool.

4. With your fingers or a knife, peel the peppers (little bits of charred skin may remain). Core the peppers and remove the seeds.

5. Use the "roasted" peppers as directed in the individual recipe or store them, covered with olive oil, in the refrigerator for up to 2 weeks.

Roasted Garlic *and* Cream Cheese Dip

Makes about 2 cups
Preparation time: 50 minutes (includes roasting the garlic) ❖ *Cooking time: None*

THE MELLOW, SUBTLE FLAVOR of roasted garlic pervades this creamy dip, making it a wonderful foil for the crispness of crudités. Our vegetables of choice are wedges of red bell pepper and spears of summer squash and zucchini.

1	8-ounce package cream cheese, softened	1	tablespoon snipped fresh chives or scallion greens
½	cup sour cream		Fresh lemon juice
½	cup drained low-fat plain yogurt (see Tip)		Salt and freshly ground black pepper
2	garlic heads, roasted (see opposite page)		Crudités, for dipping

1. In a food processor, combine the cream cheese, sour cream and yogurt. Add the roasted garlic pulp and process until smooth.

2. Transfer the mixture to a serving bowl and stir in the chives or scallions. Add lemon juice and salt and pepper to taste; combine well. Serve with the crudités.

❖ To drain yogurt, line a sieve with a piece of cheesecloth that has been rinsed and squeezed dry. Place the yogurt in the sieve set over a bowl and set aside to drain for about 20 minutes, or until the yogurt is thick. Discard the liquid in the bowl.

TO ROAST WHOLE HEADS OF GARLIC

Preparation time: 5 minutes ❖ *Cooking time: 50 minutes*

WHEN GARLIC IS ROASTED, it loses all the sharp, biting pungency that makes it so powerful when raw. Roasted garlic can be spread like butter. You can also swirl it into soups, add it to salad dressings or put it on pizza. Plan ahead. It takes nearly an hour to roast.

**Garlic heads, loose papery outer skin removed
but cloves still attached
Olive oil (1 teaspoon per garlic head)**

1. Preheat the oven to 400°F.

2. Place the garlic heads on a piece of foil and drizzle them with the oil. Wrap the garlic heads in the foil and roast for 45 to 50 minutes, or until the garlic is very soft. Let cool.

3. Pop the roasted cloves out of their skins into a bowl. Use as directed in the recipes.

Roasted Red Pepper *and* Garlic Pesto

Makes 2 cups
Preparation time: 1 hour 20 minutes (includes roasting the peppers and garlic)
Cooking time: None

THIS RECIPE TAKES PESTO, the classic basil sauce of Italy, one step farther. Our version uses roasted garlic and combines it with roasted red peppers. It's wonderful on hot pasta or roasted vegetables or with grilled fish.

2	red bell peppers, roasted (see page 39), peeled, cored and seeded	½	cup freshly grated Parmesan
1	garlic head, roasted (see page 41)	⅓	cup extra-virgin olive oil, or more to taste
2	cups loosely packed fresh basil leaves		Salt and freshly ground black pepper
½	cup toasted pine nuts (see Tip)		

In a food processor, combine the bell peppers, garlic pulp, basil, pine nuts and Parmesan and puree until smooth. With the motor running, add the ⅓ cup oil in a thin stream and process until well combined. Add a little more oil to thin, if necessary. Season with salt and pepper to taste. Store in an airtight container in the refrigerator for up to 1 week.

❖ To toast pine nuts, place them in a small, dry skillet over medium heat and toast, stirring occasionally, for 3 to 5 minutes, or until golden brown and fragrant. Remove from the skillet and let cool.

Roasted Herbed Potato Thins

Makes about 6 cups
Preparation time: 15 minutes ❖ *Cooking time: 20 minutes*

THESE POTATO THINS resemble the thick-cut chips from the supermarket, but they taste fresher and are much lower in fat. While we've chosen fresh herbs and ordinary olive oil to make them, you should feel free to vary the recipe using flavored oils. Basil oil would be good—in that event, use only fresh basil, not a combination of herbs, to garnish the chips. Garlic oil is another possibility.

If you like things hot and would like to try chili oil, replace 1 to 2 teaspoons of the ⅓ cup oil called for below with chili oil.

3 large russet or Idaho potatoes (about 2 pounds), unpeeled, cut into very thin slices (about ¹⁄₁₆ inch thick) and patted dry	⅓ cup olive oil 3 tablespoons minced fresh rosemary, oregano or thyme or a combination, or 1 tablespoon dried, crumbled Salt

1. Preheat the oven to 450°F. Lightly oil 2 baking sheets.

2. Brush both sides of the potato slices with the oil, then arrange them in a single layer on the baking sheets. Sprinkle with the herbs and salt to taste. Roast the potatoes, turning them once, for 15 to 20 minutes, or until golden brown. Let cool slightly and transfer to a serving dish. Serve warm or at room temperature.

Roasted Potato Skins *with*

Monterey Jack Cheese *and* Chipotle Chiles

Makes 24 pieces
Preparation time: 20 minutes ❖ *Cooking time: 25 minutes*

THESE STRIPS OF POTATO SKINS make a wonderful snack and can be varied in any number of ways: Top the cheese with a dab of salsa, or substitute different cheeses. The chipotle chiles en adobo—smoked jalapeños in spicy tomato sauce—lend a singular flavor typical of the Southwest. If you have never tasted them, they are well worth seeking out in Mexican or Hispanic markets or even some better-stocked supermarkets.

4   large Idaho or russet potatoes
      (2½ pounds), unpeeled,
      scrubbed and patted dry
      Salt
1½ cups grated Monterey Jack or
      Cheddar cheese (6 ounces)

2   canned chipotle chiles en adobo,
      drained and minced
1   tablespoon adobo sauce
      (from the chiles),
      or more to taste

1. Preheat the oven to 450°F. Lightly oil a baking sheet.

2. Use a paring knife to remove the skin from the potatoes in strips 1 inch wide and 3 inches long, leaving about ⅛ inch of potato flesh on each one. (Reserve the peeled potatoes, covered in water, for another use, such as mashed potatoes.)

3. Arrange the strips in a single layer in the pan and season with salt to taste. Roast for 20 minutes, or until golden and crisp.

4. In a bowl, combine the cheese, chipotle chiles and adobo sauce. Spoon some of the mixture onto each skin and roast for 5 minutes more, or until the cheese is melted. Serve at once on a platter.

Roasted Baby Potatoes *with* Scallion Cream

Makes 24 potatoes
Preparation time: 20 minutes ❖ *Cooking time: 20 minutes*

FOR THESE HOLLOWED-OUT POTATOES that make attractive finger food, you'll need to find baby potatoes. At some markets, they may be called "new potatoes," for they are harvested young and are smaller than the more common medium reds. You can make these lighter if you wish: Substitute Neufchâtel for the cream cheese and light sour cream for the real thing.

For the roasted potatoes

24 baby red potatoes, each about
   1½ inches in diameter,
   rinsed and patted dry
1 tablespoon olive oil
1 tablespoon unsalted butter, melted
1 tablespoon minced fresh rosemary,
   or 1 teaspoon dried,
   crumbled (optional)
Salt and freshly ground black pepper

For the scallion cream

1 3-ounce package cream cheese,
   softened
3 tablespoons sour cream
2 scallions, thinly sliced
Salt
Cayenne pepper

Fresh rosemary sprigs, for garnish
   (optional)

1. Preheat the oven to 450°F.

2. **Make the roasted potatoes:** Using a melon baller or a teaspoon with a serrated tip, hollow out each potato, leaving ½ inch of the shell intact; discard the pulp. In a large bowl, combine the potatoes with the oil, butter, rosemary (if using) and salt and pepper to taste. Arrange the potatoes in a single layer in a shallow roasting pan and roast, turning occasionally, for 20 minutes, or until tender and golden brown.

3. **Meanwhile, make the scallion cream:** In a small bowl, whisk the cream cheese and sour cream until smooth. Stir in the scallions and salt and cayenne to taste.

4. Spoon a dollop of the scallion cream into each potato, then arrange the potatoes on a serving plate. Garnish with sprigs of fresh rosemary, if desired.

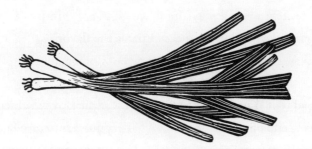

Roasted Tomato *and* Mozzarella Bruschetta

Makes 18 toasts, serving 6
Preparation time: 20 minutes ❖ *Cooking time: 13 minutes*

MOST PEOPLE KNOW BRUSCHETTA as toasted rounds of garlic bread, topped with a slice each of mozzarella and fresh tomato. In this recipe, the tomatoes are roasted and the cheese is melted, and the difference in taste, texture and pleasure is worth every minute of additional effort. Don't forego the balsamic vinegar. Like good wine, it accentuates the flavors.

Serve these with drinks as a first course, or with a bowl of homemade soup.

18	slices Italian bread (cut ½ inch thick)	3	garlic cloves, minced
2	tablespoons plus ⅓ cup olive oil	1	pound mozzarella cheese,
9	firm but ripe plum tomatoes, cored,		cut into 18 slices
	halved lengthwise and seeds removed	⅓	cup minced fresh basil
	(without crushing the flesh)		Balsamic vinegar

1. Preheat the oven to 450°F.

2. Lightly brush both sides of the bread slices with oil, using about 2 tablespoons total, and arrange in a single layer on a baking sheet.

3. Lightly oil a 9-x-13-inch baking pan. Arrange the tomato halves, cut side up, in the baking pan, sprinkle with the garlic and drizzle with the remaining ⅓ cup oil.

4. Roast the bread slices and the tomatoes for 5 to 8 minutes, or until the bread slices are golden around the edges and the tomatoes are hot and glistening. Turn the bread slices over and top each one with a piece of cheese. Roast the bread and tomatoes 3 to 5 minutes more, or until the cheese is melted.

5. Arrange the bread slices on a serving platter and top each with a roasted tomato half. Garnish with the basil and sprinkle with balsamic vinegar to taste. Serve at once.

Roasted Shrimp *and* Tomato Bruschetta

Makes 4 toasts, serving 4
Preparation time: 30 minutes ❖ *Cooking time: 20 minutes*

BRUSCHETTA CAN BE AS RUSTIC or as sophisticated as you like, these falling in the latter category. The flavors are fresh, the colors appealing and the approach straightforward. Take care not to overcook the shrimp.

4 slices country-style Italian bread (cut ½ inch thick)	3 tablespoons minced fresh basil, plus 4 whole leaves, for garnish
4 tablespoons olive oil	Salt and freshly ground black pepper
1 whole garlic clove, plus 2 teaspoons minced garlic	1 pound large shrimp, peeled and deveined
3 cups peeled, seeded and chopped plum tomatoes (6-8)	1 tablespoon balsamic vinegar

1. Preheat the broiler.

2. Lightly brush both sides of the bread with oil, using about 2 tablespoons total, and rub both sides with the whole garlic clove. Place the slices on a baking sheet and broil until lightly toasted, turning once.

3. Preheat the oven to 450°F.

4. In a skillet, heat the remaining 2 tablespoons oil over medium heat until hot. Add the minced garlic and cook, stirring, for 1 minute, or until fragrant. Add the tomatoes, 2 tablespoons of the basil and salt and pepper to taste and simmer, stirring occasionally, for 3 minutes, or until the tomatoes begin to soften.

5. Place the shrimp in a shallow baking dish, top with the tomato mixture and roast for 6 to 8 minutes, or until the shrimp are firm to the touch. Stir in the remaining 1 tablespoon basil and the vinegar.

6. Place 1 piece of bread on each serving plate, spoon an equal amount of the shrimp mixture over each one and garnish with a whole basil leaf.

*I*ndonesian Roasted Pork Cubes *with*

Peanut Dipping Sauce

Serves 6 as a first course, 4 as a main course (with rice)
Preparation time: 2 hours 20 minutes (includes marinating the pork)
Cooking time: 12 minutes

GRILLED SKEWERED meat or seafood are called satays in Indonesia and are a popular street food, grilled right in front of you at stands on street corners. We've eliminated the skewers, roasted the pork and added a sensational creamy peanut sauce, which turns this quintessential finger food into a full-flavored first course. It can also be served as an entrée with rice.

For the marinade

½ cup minced shallots (3-4 large shallots)
1 quarter-size slice fresh ginger,
   peeled and minced
2 tablespoons fresh lemon juice
2 tablespoons reduced-sodium soy sauce
2 tablespoons Asian sesame oil
2 medium garlic cloves, minced
1 teaspoon dark brown sugar
   Salt to taste
   Red pepper flakes to taste

1 pound boneless pork loin,
   cut into 1-inch cubes

For the peanut sauce

¼ cup smooth peanut butter
1 cup light cream
3 tablespoons reduced-sodium soy sauce
1 tablespoon fresh lemon juice
1 teaspoon dark brown sugar
¼ teaspoon red pepper flakes
2 tablespoons minced fresh cilantro

1. **Make the marinade:** In a large shallow bowl, combine all the marinade ingredients. Add the pork, turning to coat. Cover and refrigerate for at least 2 hours or overnight.

2. Preheat the oven to 500°F. Lightly oil a roasting pan.

3. Remove the pork from the marinade and place it in a single layer in the roasting pan. Roast for 10 to 12 minutes, or until cooked through.

4. **Meanwhile, make the peanut sauce:** In a small saucepan, combine all the ingredients except the cilantro and simmer, stirring, until smooth and heated through; do not boil. Remove from the heat and stir in the cilantro. Cover and keep warm until ready to serve, then pour into a serving bowl.

5. Transfer the pork to a serving platter and serve with toothpicks, with the peanut sauce in a bowl on the side.

Oysters Casino

Serves 4

Preparation time: 20 minutes

Cooking time: 25 minutes (includes preheating the baking dish)

THIS DISH IS MODELED AFTER the famous appetizer, clams casino. The slightly untraditional version here calls for roasting instead of the usual broiling. To prevent the oysters from wobbling, place them on a bed of rock salt. Make sure the rock salt is pure sodium chloride. *Do not use rock salts containing potassium chloride or calcium chloride; they are unsuitable for culinary purposes.* (Rock salt is available at specialty food stores and some hardware stores; one safe brand is Halite.) Kosher salt, which is much finer, will adhere to the shells and is not recommended as a substitute.

The shallots and peppers in the butter mixture topping the oysters remain slightly firm, in contrast to the plump softness of the just-heated-through bivalves. The bacon topping becomes delightfully crisp.

This is a celebratory first course, deserving of beef sirloin or tenderloin to follow (see pages 150 or 152). If oysters are not available, hard-shelled clams are an acceptable substitute.

24 oysters, shucked and on the half-shell	¼ cup finely diced green bell pepper
6 slices bacon	2 tablespoons minced fresh parsley
12 tablespoons (1½ sticks) unsalted butter, softened	1 teaspoon grated lemon zest
⅓ cup minced shallots (2-3 large shallots)	2 tablespoons fresh lemon juice
¼ cup finely diced red bell pepper	Salt and freshly ground black pepper
	2 tablespoons fresh bread crumbs

1. Preheat the oven to 500°F. Line a baking dish large enough to hold the oysters in a single layer with rock salt and heat in the oven for 10 minutes.

2. Meanwhile, in a large skillet, cook the bacon, turning once, over medium heat until slightly crisped. Drain on paper towels. Cut into 24 pieces.

3. In a small bowl, with a spoon, combine the butter, shallots, bell peppers, parsley, lemon zest, juice and salt and pepper to taste. Top each oyster with some of the butter mixture, then top with a piece of the cooked bacon and sprinkle with some of the bread crumbs.

4. Arrange the oysters on the salt in the preheated baking dish and roast for 8 minutes, or until heated through and the bacon is crisp. Wearing an oven mitt, arrange the hot oysters on serving plates and serve at once.

Roasted Garlic *and* Goat Cheese Flans *with* Roasted Red Pepper Sauce

Serves 6

Preparation time: 1¼ hours (includes roasting the garlic and making the sauce)

Cooking time: 25 minutes

THESE TENDER CUSTARDS make a superb first course for a dinner of Roasted Peppered Tenderloin of Beef with Port Wine Sauce (page 152). Although best served straight from the oven, the flans can be held for 30 minutes in the water bath.

2	garlic heads, roasted (see page 41)	4	large eggs
1	pound Montrachet, Bucheron or other mild goat cheese (the type not coated with ash), diced	2	tablespoons snipped fresh chives
			Salt and freshly ground black pepper
			Roasted Red Pepper Sauce

1. Preheat the oven to 350°F. Generously butter six ½-cup ramekins.

2. In a food processor, combine the roasted garlic pulp, goat cheese, eggs, chives and salt and pepper to taste; process until smooth.

3. Divide the mixture among the ramekins. Set the ramekins in a shallow baking pan and add just enough hot water to the pan to reach halfway up the sides of the ramekins. Bake for 20 to 25 minutes, or until puffed and golden.

4. Gently heat the sauce and spoon a pool into the middle of each serving plate, then invert and unmold each flan onto the sauce. Pass any remaining sauce at the table.

ROASTED RED PEPPER SAUCE

Makes 1½ cups to 2 cups (if the optional ingredients are used)
Preparation time: 20 minutes (includes roasting the peppers)
Cooking time: None

WE ESPECIALLY LIKE this beautifully colored sauce on stuffed chicken breasts and roasted fish fillets. It also makes a good dipping sauce for roasted vegetables, and it is perfect with Roasted Garlic and Goat Cheese Flans (opposite page).

3	large red bell peppers, roasted (see page 39), peeled, cored and seeded, juice reserved
3	tablespoons extra-virgin olive oil
1	tablespoon fresh lemon juice, or more to taste
	Salt
	Cayenne pepper
3-4	tablespoons heavy cream, sour cream or plain yogurt (optional)
2	tablespoons minced fresh basil, dill or tarragon (optional)

1. In a food processor or blender, combine the peppers with their reserved juice and puree until smooth. Add the oil, 1 tablespoon lemon juice and salt and cayenne to taste and process until combined. Taste and add more lemon juice, if desired.

2. Transfer to a serving bowl and stir in the cream, sour cream or yogurt and herbs, if using. Store in an airtight container in the refrigerator. If made without dairy products, the sauce will keep for up to 1 week; with dairy products, it will keep for up to 3 days.

Chapter II

Soups

WHY TAKE THE ADDITIONAL STEP OF ROASTING an ingredient for the soup pot? The simple reason is the flavor factor. Sautéing cannot produce a comparable result, nor can simply simmering vegetables in liquid. Roasting adds complexity.

The heat of the oven evaporates liquid in vegetables, which generally have a high water content, concentrating their essence. A zucchini that has been roasted is burnished outside, firm and flavorful; one that has been simmered tastes bland and waterlogged. Vegetables high in sugar, like leeks and onions, are caramelized in the roasting process, which highlights their natural sweetness.

Though this extra step does take a little more time, the technique itself is kind to the cook. The vegetables are placed in a shallow roasting pan, sometimes tossed with a minimum of oil to facilitate browning, and roasted, essentially unattended, save for an occasional stir. When they are browned and tender, they are combined with liquid, preferably homemade stock, and the remaining ingredients are added to the pot to simmer for a brief period of time to blend the flavors. The soup is then either pureed, resulting in a creamy texture, or served as is for a heartier presentation.

Roasted Eggplant and Red Pepper Soup with Pistou (page 65) typifies the fullness of flavor that can be achieved when eggplant, onion, red peppers, tomatoes and garlic are roasted with herbs. The one cold soup in this chapter, Chilled Roasted Red Pepper Soup with Feta and Dill (page 78), depends upon the haunting flavor of bell peppers that have been charred until black, then peeled and pureed. Curried Butternut Squash Soup with Cilantro Cream (page 62) and Roasted Pumpkin Soup with Gruyère and Parmesan Croûtes (page 70) are luxurious-tasting but contain neither heavy cream nor the double indemnity of heavy cream and egg yolks.

These recipes lend themselves to being made in stages, a practical consideration when they are to be served during the week.

Soups

Curried Butternut Squash Soup

with Cilantro Cream

Makes 6½ cups, serving 4
Preparation time: 20 minutes (does not include making the Cilantro Cream)
Cooking time: 45 minutes

THE COMBINATION OF CURRY POWDER, GINGER AND CAYENNE gives this soup an exotic flavor, and the Cilantro Cream makes it especially pretty. The soup can be served hot or chilled. If you prefer a smooth texture, puree it in a blender instead of a food processor.

1	medium butternut squash (1½ pounds)	5	cups homemade or canned chicken stock
2	tablespoons vegetable oil	1	bay leaf
1	large onion, minced	1	teaspoon salt, or more to taste
2	garlic cloves, minced		Pinch of cayenne pepper, or more to taste
2	teaspoons minced fresh ginger		
1	tablespoon curry powder, or more to taste	1½	tablespoons fresh lemon juice
1	tablespoon flour		Cilantro Cream (page 64), for topping

1. Preheat the oven to 400°F. Lightly oil a baking sheet.

2. Halve the squash lengthwise and remove the seeds, discarding any strings. (Reserve the squash seeds for slow-roasting, following the directions on page 71.) Place the squash, cut side down, on the baking sheet and roast for 30 to 35 minutes, or until the flesh is tender when tested with a fork. Let cool. Scoop out the flesh from the skin into a bowl; set aside. Discard the skin.

3. Meanwhile, in a large saucepan, heat the oil over medium heat until hot. Add the onion, garlic and ginger and cook, stirring occasionally, for 3 minutes, or until the onion is slightly softened. Add the curry powder and flour and cook, stirring, for 2 minutes, to toast the curry. Add the stock, bay leaf, salt and cayenne, bring to a boil and simmer over medium-low heat, stirring occasionally, for 20 minutes to blend the flavors. Remove and discard the bay leaf.

4. In a food processor or blender, combine the roasted squash and 2 cups of the stock mixture and process until smooth. Transfer to a large, clean saucepan. Puree the remaining stock mixture and add it to the saucepan.

5. Bring the soup to a simmer, stirring, and season with the lemon juice and additional salt and cayenne to taste if necessary. Ladle into heated bowls and top each serving with a spoonful of the cilantro cream.

Cilantro Cream

Makes about 1 cup
Preparation time: 10 minutes ❖ *Cooking time: None*

I F YOU WANT TO MAKE AN ATTRACTIVE DESIGN on the surface of the soup, put the cilantro cream into a plastic squirt bottle—the kind mustard and ketchup are frequently served in.

½   cup heavy cream
¼   cup sour cream
¼   cup minced fresh cilantro
        Salt and freshly ground black pepper

In a small bowl, combine the cream, sour cream and cilantro. Season with salt and white pepper to taste. The cream can be prepared up to 2 hours in advance and kept, covered and chilled, until serving time.

$\mathcal{R}$oasted Eggplant *and* Red Pepper Soup

with Pistou

Makes 9 cups, serving 6
Preparation time: 20 minutes (includes making the pistou)
Cooking time: 1 hour 20 minutes

HERE IS A LOVELY END-OF-THE-SUMMER, harvest-type soup that, depending upon the weather, you can serve warm, as suggested below, or cold, with a dollop of plain yogurt. Pistou, the famous Provençal basil and garlic sauce, is a memorable topping. Add a loaf of crusty bread and a small salad and you have the makings of a very fine light lunch or late supper.

1	large eggplant (about 1½ pounds), halved lengthwise	1	teaspoon dried, crumbled rosemary
1	large onion, quartered	½	teaspoon dried, crumbled thyme
3	tablespoons olive oil	½	teaspoon dried, crumbled basil
2	red bell peppers, cored, seeded and quartered		Salt and freshly ground black pepper
2	tomatoes, cored, halved and seeded	6	cups homemade or canned chicken stock
2	large garlic cloves		Pistou (page 67), for topping

1. Preheat the oven to 425°F. Lightly oil a shallow baking pan large enough to hold all the vegetables in a single layer.

2. Place the eggplant, cut side down, and the onion in the baking pan. Drizzle with 2 tablespoons of the oil and roast for 20 minutes, or until lightly browned.

3. Add the remaining 1 tablespoon oil, the bell peppers, tomatoes, garlic, rosemary, thyme, basil and salt and pepper to taste to the baking pan, toss the vegetables with the pan juices and bake for 20 to 25 minutes, or until tender.

4. Scoop out the flesh from the skin of the eggplant, discard the skin and chop the eggplant and the other vegetables.

5. In a large saucepan, combine the eggplant and other vegetables with the stock and season with salt and pepper to taste. Bring to a boil and simmer, stirring occasionally, for 30 minutes.

6. In a food processor or blender, puree the soup in batches. Return the puree to the saucepan and simmer for 5 minutes, or until heated through. Serve in heated bowls topped with the pistou.

Pistou

Makes about ¾ cup

Preparation time: 5 minutes ❖ *Cooking time: None*

LIKE ITALIAN PESTO, PISTOU DEPENDS UPON FRESH BASIL. If you grow your own, you can make up a batch of this full-flavored French sauce at any time during the summer. If you have the time, grind the basil, garlic and Parmesan to a paste with a mortar and pestle, the traditional implements for making pistou. Use high-quality extra-virgin olive oil for the best flavor.

> 1½ cups fresh basil leaves
>
> 4 large garlic cloves, chopped
>
> ⅓ cup freshly grated Parmesan
>
> Salt and freshly ground black pepper
>
> ½ cup extra-virgin olive oil

1. In a food processor or blender, puree the basil, garlic and Parmesan, scraping down the sides with a spatula. Add salt and pepper to taste.

2. With the motor running, add the oil, scraping down the sides, and process the mixture until well combined. Transfer the pistou to a serving bowl.

Roasted Onion *and* Leek Soup

Makes 12 cups, serving 6 to 8
Preparation time: 20 minutes (does not include making the croûtes)
Cooking time: 1 hour

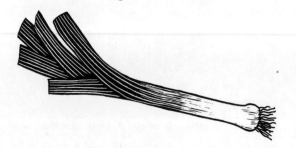

A CROCK OF CLASSIC FRENCH ONION SOUP, with its cheese-encrusted croûte, is a winter indulgence, guaranteed to warm the body as it soothes the soul. Here is an equally satisfying onion soup for all seasons. It is simpler, lighter and a little sweet too, because of the addition of leeks. The onions should roast only until golden; you do not want them to singe around the edges, which would add a burned flavor to the stock.

Serve for lunch with a vegetable salad, as a first course or as an easy supper. It freezes very well.

3 pounds onions (10-12), sliced ½ inch thick	1 cup dry white wine
2 pounds leeks (8-10), white and light green parts, washed and cut into 1-inch pieces	6-8 cups homemade or canned beef stock
2 tablespoons olive oil	1 sprig fresh thyme, or 1 teaspoon dried, crumbled
Salt and freshly ground black pepper	1 bay leaf
	Gruyère and Parmesan Croûtes (page 72)

1. Preheat the oven to 425°F.

2. In a large roasting pan, toss the onions and leeks with the oil and season with salt and pepper to taste. Roast, stirring often, for 30 minutes, or until the onions are golden. (Do not let them get crispy around the edges.) Transfer to a large pot.

3. Pour the wine into the roasting pan. Bring to a boil over high heat, scraping up the browned bits. Boil for 1 minute, then add to the onions and leeks. Add 6 cups of the stock, the thyme, bay leaf and salt and pepper to taste and bring to a boil. Reduce the heat to low and simmer for 30 minutes to concentrate the flavors, adding some or all of the remaining 2 cups stock as needed if the soup becomes too thick. Remove and discard the thyme sprig, if used, and the bay leaf.

4. Ladle the soup into heated bowls and top each with a hot cheese croûte.

Roasted Pumpkin Soup

with Gruyère *and* Parmesan Croûtes

Makes 18 cups, serving 10 to 12

Preparation time: 20 minutes (does not include making the croûtes)

Cooking time: 55 minutes

IF YOU HAVE BEEN LUCKY ENOUGH to taste fresh pumpkin soup, the pumpkin was probably initially sautéed in butter and the soup enriched with heavy cream—delicious but hardly low-fat. Here the pumpkin is roasted, giving it an almost nutty flavor, and stock replaces cream—the result being intensely flavorful, but better for you.

The yield is generous: Freeze what you don't need. This is a marvelous offering for a cool-weather open house. Serve it in a hollowed-out partially steamed pumpkin shell for an arresting presentation. If you don't have time to make the cheese croûtes, garnish the soup with roasted pumpkin seeds instead.

1   5-to-6-pound sugar pumpkin or similar pumpkin, quartered and seeded, seeds reserved for slow-roasting, if desired (see Tip)

2   tablespoons unsalted butter

1   large onion, minced

½   cup minced celery

4   garlic cloves, minced

6-8   cups homemade or canned chicken stock

1   sprig fresh thyme, or 1 teaspoon dried, crumbled

1   bay leaf
   Salt and freshly ground black pepper
   Gruyère and Parmesan Croûtes
   (page 72)

1. Preheat the oven to 400°F. Lightly oil a baking sheet.

2. Place the pumpkin pieces, cut side down, on the baking sheet and roast for 25 to 30 minutes, or until the flesh is tender when tested with a fork. Let cool, then scoop out the flesh; discard the shell.

3. Meanwhile, in a large saucepan, melt the butter over medium heat. Add the onion, celery and garlic and cook, stirring occasionally, for 5 to 7 minutes, or until the onion is lightly golden. Add 6 cups of the stock, the thyme, bay leaf and salt and pepper to taste and simmer for 20 minutes.

4. Add the pumpkin to the stock mixture. Simmer for 15 minutes. Remove and discard the thyme sprig (if used) and the bay leaf.

5. In a food processor or blender, puree the soup in batches. Return the puree to the saucepan. If the soup is too thick, thin with some or all of the remaining 2 cups stock. Correct the seasonings and heat until hot.

6. Ladle the soup into heated bowls and top each with a hot cheese croûte.

❖ **To slow-roast pumpkin seeds, wash the seeds, then pat dry with paper towels. Spread the seeds on an oiled baking sheet and roast in a preheated 250°F oven, stirring occasionally, for 50 to 60 minutes, or until lightly colored. Sprinkle with coarse salt, if desired, and let cool. Store in an airtight container.**

GRUYÈRE AND PARMESAN CROÛTES

Makes 12

Preparation time: 10 minutes ❖ *Cooking time: 11 minutes*

FLOAT THESE TOASTS on Roasted Pumpkin Soup (page 70) or Roasted Onion and Leek Soup (page 68). They make a fitting accompaniment to Roasted Vegetable Soup with Savoy Cabbage and Pasta (page 76) as well.

12	slices Italian or French bread, cut ½ inch thick on the diagonal
2	large garlic cloves, halved
2	tablespoons extra-virgin olive oil
1	cup grated Gruyère cheese
½	cup freshly grated Parmesan

1. Preheat the oven to 400°F.

2. Rub both sides of each slice of bread with the garlic and brush with the oil. Arrange the slices on a baking sheet and bake, turning once, for 7 minutes total, or until lightly toasted. Spoon some of both cheeses over each slice and bake for 3 to 4 minutes, or until the cheeses are melted. Serve at once.

$\mathcal{R}$oasted Tomato Soup *with* Basmati Rice

Makes 6 cups, serving 4
Preparation time: 15 minutes ❖ *Cooking time: 50 minutes*

LIGHT AND REFRESHING, this soup has a hint of orange. Serve hot or chilled.

6	large tomatoes (3-3½ pounds), cored and halved	1	teaspoon dried thyme
			Salt and freshly ground black pepper
2	leeks, white and pale green parts, quartered and washed	2	cups homemade or canned chicken stock
4	garlic cloves	⅓	cup basmati rice, well washed
2	tablespoons olive oil	½	teaspoon grated orange zest
1	teaspoon dried basil	3	tablespoons minced fresh basil

1. Preheat the oven to 450°F.

2. In a large roasting pan, combine the tomatoes, leeks and garlic. Add the oil, dried basil, thyme and salt and pepper to taste; toss to combine. Roast for 30 minutes, turning the vegetables once, or until soft.

3. In a food processor or blender, puree the roasted vegetables in batches, adding some of the chicken stock to each batch. Force the puree through a medium sieve or a food mill into a large saucepan.

4. Add additional stock to the saucepan, if needed to thin the mixture, and bring to a simmer. Add the rice, orange zest and salt and pepper to taste. Simmer, stirring occasionally, for 20 minutes, or until the rice is tender.

5. Stir in the fresh basil and ladle the soup into bowls.

Roasted Sweet Potato
and White Bean Chowder *with* Sage

Makes 10 cups, serving 6
Preparation time: Overnight (using the long-soak method for the beans)
or 1½ hours (using the quick-soak method)
Cooking time: 1¼ hours

THIS SOUP IS BEAUTIFUL, with a velvety puree studded with beans and pieces of roasted sweet potatoes. It is a delicious way to increase your intake of beta-carotene, since sweet potatoes are high in that important antioxidant.

Serve with bread sticks and a salad for lunch. And while the bacon adds a splendid smoky note, if you'd rather not use it, chop scallions, both green and white parts, and sprinkle them generously over the soup with the parsley.

For the beans, you can use either the quick-soak or the overnight method. Both are described below.

1 cup dried white beans, picked over	4 garlic cloves, chopped
2 pounds (4 medium to large) sweet potatoes	Freshly ground black pepper
1 onion, studded with 3 whole cloves, plus 1½ cups chopped onions (about 2)	6 cups homemade or canned chicken stock
Salt	1 bay leaf
¼ pound thick-sliced bacon	2 teaspoons minced fresh sage, or 1 teaspoon dried, crumbled
½ cup chopped celery	Cayenne pepper
	3 tablespoons minced fresh parsley

1. Soak the beans overnight in water to cover and drain. Or, to quick-soak the beans, place them in a large pot, cover with 2 inches of water and bring to a boil; boil for 2 minutes. Remove from the heat and let soak for 1 hour. Drain.

2. Preheat the oven to 425°F.

3. Roast the sweet potatoes on the oven rack for 30 to 40 minutes, or until just fork-tender. Let cool, then peel and dice. Cover and set aside.

4. Meanwhile, in a large saucepan, combine the drained beans with the clove-studded onion and enough water to cover by 2 inches. Bring to a simmer and cook, stirring occasionally, for 30 minutes, or until tender. During the last 10 minutes of cooking, add salt to taste. Drain the beans and set aside; discard the onion.

5. In a large skillet, cook the bacon over medium heat until crisp. Drain on paper towels, crumble and set aside. Pour off all but 2 tablespoons fat from the pan. Add the chopped onions, celery, garlic and salt and pepper to taste and cook, stirring occasionally, for 5 minutes, or until the vegetables are softened. Add the stock, bay leaf, sage and cayenne to taste and simmer for 15 minutes, or until the flavors are beginning to blend.

6. Add two thirds of the sweet potatoes and simmer for 15 minutes more, or until all the vegetables are tender. Discard the bay leaf.

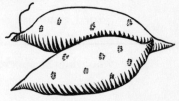

7. In a food processor or blender, puree the soup in batches, and return it to the pan. Stir in the cooked beans, the remaining sweet potatoes and salt and pepper to taste. Cook, stirring, over medium heat until hot.

8. Ladle the chowder into heated bowls and garnish with the crumbled bacon and parsley.

Roasted Vegetable Soup *with*

Savoy Cabbage *and* Pasta

Makes 8 cups, serving 6 to 8
Preparation time: 30 minutes (includes making the broth)
Cooking time: 2 hours 40 minutes

THIS VEGETARIAN SOUP is similar to minestrone. Pistou, an intense pestolike sauce, adds good garlicky flavor.

For the vegetable broth

4	large onions, quartered
2	carrots, peeled and quartered
6	large garlic cloves
1	tablespoon olive oil
1	large sprig thyme, or 1 teaspoon dried, crumbled
1	large sprig rosemary, or 1 teaspoon dried, crumbled
1	bay leaf
12	whole black peppercorns
6	whole cloves
2	tablespoons tomato paste

For the soup

4	onions, quartered
2	carrots, peeled and quartered
1	small celery root, peeled and quartered (see Tip)
6	garlic cloves
1	sprig fresh thyme, or 1 teaspoon dried, crumbled
1	tablespoon vegetable oil
2	cups shredded savoy cabbage
1	cup small pasta shells
1	tablespoon white wine vinegar
	Salt and freshly ground black pepper

Pistou (page 67), for serving
Freshly grated Parmesan, for serving

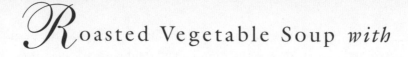

1. **Make the vegetable broth:** Preheat the oven to 400°F. In a roasting pan, combine the onions, carrots and garlic. Add the oil and toss to coat. Roast, stirring once, for 45 minutes, or until golden brown and tender.

2. In a large saucepan, combine the roasted vegetables, 3 quarts water, the thyme, rosemary, bay leaf, peppercorns, cloves and tomato paste. Bring to a boil and simmer, stirring occasionally, for 1 hour, or until the broth is reduced to about 8 cups. Strain. (The broth may be prepared 1 or 2 days in advance: cool, cover and refrigerate. The broth may also be frozen for up to 1 month.)

3. **Make the soup:** Preheat the oven to 400°F. In a large roasting pan, combine the onions, carrots, celery root, garlic and thyme. Add the oil and toss to coat. Roast, stirring twice, for 45 minutes, or until golden brown and tender. Let cool slightly, then cut the vegetables into bite-size pieces and chop the garlic.

4. In a large saucepan, bring the vegetable broth to a boil. Add the cabbage and pasta and simmer, stirring occasionally, for 10 minutes. Add the vegetables, vinegar and salt and pepper to taste and simmer until the cabbage and pasta are tender. Remove the bay leaf and the thyme sprig, if used.

5. Ladle the soup into heated bowls and garnish each serving with a spoonful or two of the pistou and a sprinkling of the Parmesan.

❖ **Also called celeriac, celery root is a knobby root that tastes like a combination of celery and parsley. Look for it in the produce section. It must be peeled and should be dropped into acidulated water to keep it from discoloring.**

Chilled Roasted Red Pepper Soup

with Feta *and* Dill

Makes 9½ cups, serving 6 to 8
Preparation time: 25 minutes (includes roasting the peppers) ❖ *Cooking time: 40 minutes*

THIS SIMPLE ROASTED RED BELL PEPPER PUREE thinned with chicken stock has two glorious characteristics: purity of flavor and gorgeous color, both attributable to the number of red peppers it contains. The better the stock, the better the soup. The time to buy bell peppers, for both best price and best quality, is the height of summer. The soup is a fine dinner party starter, as it must be prepared in advance in order to chill.

2 tablespoons olive oil	1 boiling potato, cubed
1 onion, minced	1 bay leaf
2 large garlic cloves, minced	1 sprig fresh thyme, or 1 teaspoon
1 celery stalk, minced	dried, crumbled
1 small carrot, minced	Salt and freshly ground black pepper
5 cups homemade or canned	½ cup low-fat plain yogurt or sour cream
chicken stock	½ cup crumbled feta cheese
6 red bell peppers, roasted (see page 39),	(about 2 ounces), see Tip
peeled, cored, seeded and chopped	2 tablespoons snipped fresh dill

1. In a large saucepan, heat the oil over medium heat until hot. Add the onion, garlic, celery and carrot and cook, stirring occasionally, for 5 minutes, or until the vegetables are softened. Add the stock, roasted peppers, potato, bay leaf, thyme and salt and pepper to taste. Bring to a boil and simmer, stirring occasionally, for 30 minutes. Remove and discard the bay leaf and the thyme sprig, if used.

2. In a food processor or blender, puree the soup in batches. Transfer it to a large bowl. Chill, covered, for at least 2 hours.

3. Before serving, stir in the yogurt or sour cream and correct the seasonings, adding more salt and pepper to taste. Ladle the soup into chilled bowls and garnish each serving with some of the feta and dill.

❖ **Crumbled goat cheese (not the type coated with ash) makes a good substitute for the feta.**

Chapter III

Shellfish *and* Fish

ANYONE VERSED IN COOKING SHELLFISH OR FISH knows the cardinal rule: Do not overcook it. Proceed carefully and cautiously, and err on the side of slightly underdone. To overlook this warning invariably means dry fish or tough, rubbery shellfish. Dare we, then, extol the glories of roasted shellfish and fish when the consequences can be so disappointing to the palate and disastrous to the purse?

We do—with one caveat. When your oven is set at 500°F, as it is for many of the recipes in this chapter, do not let yourself be distracted by anything else, or risk an additional minute or two of cooking, thinking it won't make a difference. It will.

The recipes that follow are some of the most special and elegant in this book. Soft-shell crabs are one of the last great seasonal specialties. Roasting them is much simpler than frying—no grease, no spattering—and the dry oven heat crisps them without obscuring their delicate flavor. Sea Scallops Roasted in Bacon (page 85) stands apart as a party dish that is virtually foolproof, since the bacon wrap on each scallop bastes and insulates it. Another showcase dinner, Roasted Lobster with Tomato and Basil Essence (page 90), has spectacular flavor; roasting delivers a quantifiably better result than boiling.

A whole roasted fish is every bit as celebratory as lobster. Roasted Red Snapper Greek Style (page 100) is quick to prepare and has just enough seasoning to highlight the fish. Roasted Sea Bass with Bread Stuffing (page 102), on the other hand, is more elaborate, both in preparation and presentation. Either recipe can be adapted to a variety of fish, including bluefish, trout, mackerel and grouper. Cooking times will vary, depending upon the size of the fish you are roasting.

When buying whole fish of any kind, there is only a single rule of thumb: Purchase the freshest one you can. It should have clear—not cloudy or filmy—eyes and a smell of the sea. Buy it at the last minute if possible. The better you know your fish market, the better your chances of getting really fresh fish.

The cooking times for fish steaks, fillets and shellfish are all short. The fillet of a naturally oily fish, like bluefish, is less susceptible to drying out than is that of a lean white-fleshed fish, like sole. Firmer-fleshed fish steaks, such as red snapper, tuna, salmon, swordfish, halibut and cod, also make for trouble-free roasting. A delicate, thin fillet is somewhat riskier to roast, because it has little fat to protect it.

For juicy and flavorful results,
keep these tips in mind when you roast:

Shellfish: To decrease the risk of overcooking, choose jumbo over medium-sized shrimp and sea scallops over bay scallops. Or, in the case of shrimp, you can roast them in the shell, which not only adds flavor, but serves to insulate them from the heat as well.

Whole Fish: Basting a whole fish once or twice during roasting helps to ensure even color as it moistens the flesh. If you are roasting more than one fish at a time, take care not to crowd them, allowing two to three inches of space between so that the heat flows evenly and they don't steam instead of roast.

Fish Steaks: Choose fish steaks that are at least one inch thick. Either brush them with olive oil or melted butter to facilitate coloring and keep them moist, or consider glazing them with hoisin sauce (see Roasted Salmon Steaks with Hoisin Glaze, page 101). Another method for ensuring moistness is to add a protective coating to seal in the juices, as in Roasted Halibut Steaks with Herbed Potato Crust (page 96).

Fillets: The guiding principle is know your fish and cook it carefully. For extra protection against the searing oven heat, you may want to add a coating of seasoned bread crumbs, like the one for Roasted Curried Bluefish Fillets (page 94).

A final word on the roasting of shellfish and fish: With the exception of the whole fish, all of the recipes in this chapter cook in 15 minutes or less.

Shellfish *and* Fish

*S*ea Scallops Roasted *in* Bacon

Serves 4

Preparation time: 40 minutes (includes marinating the scallops) ❖ *Cooking time: 15 minutes*

WRAPPED IN BACON AND ROASTED for 15 minutes, scallops stay moist, basted by the bacon, while the bacon crisps up nicely around them. The marinade adds a subtle Asian flavor and can be made spicier with more red pepper flakes.

Serve with Roasted Sugar Snap Peas (page 194) and Roasted Carrots with Ginger (page 178) for an attractive presentation.

For the marinade
- ¼ cup reduced-sodium soy sauce
- 2 tablespoons dark brown sugar
- 2 tablespoons dry sherry
- 1 tablespoon Dijon mustard
- 1 tablespoon Asian sesame oil
- 2 teaspoons minced fresh ginger

- ⅛ teaspoon red pepper flakes
- Salt to taste

For the scallops
- 24 large sea scallops, rinsed and muscle removed if necessary
- 8 slices bacon, each slice cut into thirds

1. **Make the marinade:** In a bowl, combine all the marinade ingredients. Add the scallops and stir to coat. Cover and marinate in the refrigerator for 30 minutes.

2. Preheat the oven to 450°F.

3. **Prepare the scallops:** Drain the scallops, reserving the marinade, and wrap each one in a piece of the bacon, securing it with a toothpick. Arrange the scallops on a rack in a shallow roasting pan and roast, turning frequently and basting with the reserved marinade, for 15 minutes, or until the bacon is crisp and the scallops are just cooked. Serve immediately.

Roasted Scallops *with* Leeks *and* Fennel

Serves 4

Preparation time: 30 minutes (includes roasting the pepper) ❖ *Cooking time: 15 minutes*

THIS DINNER-PARTY DISH is as easy to make as it is good to eat. Serve it with green and white fettuccine. You can substitute peeled and deveined extra-large shrimp for the scallops. Avoid bay scallops: They are too small to withstand the high heat of roasting and will turn into unappealing little pellets.

2	tablespoons olive oil	1	cup well-drained diced roasted red bell peppers from 2 medium peppers (see page 39)
1	cup julienned well-washed leeks		
½	cup julienned fennel bulb		
½	cup julienned carrot	½	cup diced pitted kalamata olives
1	garlic clove, minced	3	tablespoons minced fresh basil or parsley
	Salt and freshly ground black pepper	1½	pounds sea scallops, rinsed, muscle removed if necessary and halved if large

1. Preheat the oven to 450°F. Lightly oil an 8-x-12-inch gratin dish.

2. In a medium saucepan, heat the 2 tablespoons oil over medium-high heat until hot. Add the leeks, fennel, carrot, garlic and salt and pepper to taste and cook, covered, for 5 minutes, or until the vegetables are softened. Transfer the vegetables to a bowl and stir in the red peppers, olives and 2 tablespoons of the basil or parsley.

3. Arrange half the mixture in the gratin dish; arrange the scallops in a single layer on the vegetables, and sprinkle with salt and pepper to taste. Top with the remaining vegetable mixture.

4. Roast for 8 to 10 minutes, or until the scallops are firm but still springy to the touch.

5. With a slotted spoon, divide the scallops and vegetables among heated serving plates, and sprinkle a little of the remaining 1 tablespoon fresh basil or parsley over each serving.

*R*oasted Soft-Shell Crabs *with*

Creole Tartar Sauce

Serves 4, makes 2 cups sauce
Preparation time: 1 hour 15 minutes (includes soaking the crabs and making the sauce)
Cooking time: 10 minutes

DON'T EXPECT THESE ROASTED SOFT-SHELL CRABS to be as crisp as the ones that are deep-fried. But they are just as good. The crabs are dunked in butter, then dredged in cornmeal. Don't be light-handed in either of these steps. Using ample butter ensures that the coating will adhere and become crisp.

Creole seasoning, a spicy blend, is available in the spice section of most supermarkets.

For the crabs

1	cup buttermilk
2-3	tablespoons Creole seasoning, or to taste
1	large garlic clove, minced
½	teaspoon salt
8	soft-shell crabs, cleaned (see Tip)
1½	cups yellow cornmeal
6-8	tablespoons (¾-1 stick) unsalted butter, melted

For the Creole tartar sauce

1½	cups mayonnaise
3	tablespoons minced sweet pickled gherkins
2	tablespoons minced scallions
2	teaspoons Dijon mustard
1½	teaspoons Creole seasoning
2	scant tablespoons fresh lemon juice
1-2	tablespoons minced fresh parsley

1. **Prepare the crabs:** In a wide, shallow dish, combine the buttermilk with 1 tablespoon of the Creole seasoning, the garlic and salt. Add the crabs, cover and refrigerate for 1 hour, turning once. Drain and pat dry.

2. **Meanwhile, make the Creole tartar sauce:** In a medium bowl, combine all the sauce ingredients. Transfer to a serving bowl, cover and chill.

3. Preheat the oven to 500°F. Lightly oil a baking sheet.

4. In another wide, shallow dish, combine the cornmeal with the remaining Creole seasoning. Put the butter in another wide, shallow dish. Dip the crabs, one at a time, into the melted butter, then dredge in the cornmeal, covering completely and patting to make the meal adhere. Arrange the crabs on the baking sheet and roast for 4 to 5 minutes on each side, or until golden brown and cooked through. (When the crabs are pierced, the meat should be opaque.)

5. Arrange the crabs on a platter and serve with the tartar sauce.

❖ **To clean soft-shell crabs, remove the apron-shaped tab from under the body, then lift up the sides of the body and remove the gills with scissors, or pull them off with your fingers. Slice off the front of the crab (the part with the eyes and the mouth) and remove the small sac from the head. Or you can ask to have the crabs cleaned at the fish store. Cook cleaned crabs as soon as possible; they do not keep.**

Roasted Lobster *with* Tomato *and* Basil Essence

Serves 2 as an entrée or 4 as an appetizer, makes 1 cup tomato essence
Preparation time: 25 minutes
Cooking time: 25 minutes (includes making the essence)

WHEN IT COMES TO ELEGANCE, few entrées surpass lobster. Inevitably, there comes the question of how to cook it in the most humane manner. Here, it is boiled briefly to kill it, then split and roasted. Finally, the lobsters are sauced with an intense distillation of fresh summer tomatoes and fresh basil. Roasting the lobsters not only provides a fuller flavor and better texture but also eliminates the water that inevitably spills out when you crack their shells.

This needs only crusty bread, a simple salad and a crisp white wine. For dessert, serve flourless chocolate cake.

For the lobsters

2   1½-pound lobsters
2   tablespoons unsalted butter, melted
1   tablespoon olive oil
1   tablespoon fresh lemon juice
    Salt and freshly ground black pepper

For the tomato and basil essence

6   plum tomatoes (¾-1 pound total)
2   garlic cloves, minced
2   tablespoons extra-virgin olive oil
1   tablespoon balsamic vinegar
2   tablespoons minced fresh basil, parsley
      or chives, or a combination
    Salt and freshly ground black pepper

    Minced fresh basil, for garnish

1. **Prepare the lobsters:** Preheat the oven to 450°F. Lightly oil a roasting pan.

2. Bring a large pot of salted water to a boil. Add the live lobsters, head first, and boil them for no more than 1 minute. Remove the lobsters with tongs and let drain until cool enough to handle. Split each lobster lengthwise, discarding the sac from the head and tomalley. Arrange the lobster halves, shell side down, in the roasting pan and drizzle the cut sides with the butter, oil, lemon juice and salt and pepper to taste. Roast for 12 to 15 minutes, or until the tail meat is just firm but still springy to the touch. Transfer the lobsters to a platter, cover loosely with aluminum foil and set aside to keep warm.

3. **Meanwhile, make the tomato and basil essence:** Using a long-handled fork, roast each tomato over an open flame, turning frequently, for 1 to 2 minutes, or until charred all over. Alternatively, preheat the broiler. Arrange the tomatoes in an oiled roasting pan, place 4 inches from the broiler and broil, turning, until the tomatoes are evenly charred on all sides, about 6 to 8 minutes. Let cool, then core, peel, seed and chop.

4. In a food processor or blender, combine the tomatoes, garlic, oil, vinegar, fresh herb of choice and salt and pepper to taste; process until well combined.

5. Spoon the sauce over the lobsters, garnish with the minced basil and serve.

Roasted Shrimp *in* Lemony Garlic Butter

Serves 4

Preparation time: 20 minutes ❖ *Cooking time: 10 minutes*

CALL THIS SHRIMP SCAMPI, if you like. The combination—shrimp, garlic, butter and lemon—is a classic. You will need good crusty bread to soak up the butter sauce.

Jumbo shrimp are done when they turn pinkish red. They will also feel firm to the touch. Because they are cooked on the highest heat possible, you may want to slightly undercook them—you can always put them back in the oven. Not even garlic butter, good as it is, can salvage overdone shrimp.

4	tablespoons (½ stick) unsalted butter	3	garlic cloves, mashed to a paste
¼	cup olive oil		Salt and freshly ground black pepper
1	teaspoon grated lemon zest	24	jumbo shrimp, split lengthwise and
2	tablespoons fresh lemon juice		deveined, shells left on
		3	tablespoons minced fresh parsley

1. Preheat the oven to 500°F.

2. In a small saucepan, melt the butter. Stir in the oil, zest, lemon juice, garlic and salt and pepper to taste. Remove from the heat.

3. Dip the shrimp in the garlic butter, then arrange them, split side down, with the tails pointing up, in a single layer in a shallow baking dish. Roast for 8 to 10 minutes, or until just cooked.

4. Arrange the shrimp on a serving platter, pour the cooking juices over them and sprinkle with the minced parsley. Serve at once.

$\mathcal{R}$oasted Cod Steaks *with* Corn Salsa

Serves 4

Preparation time: 1¼ hours (includes making and chilling the salsa)

Cooking time: 12 minutes

ROASTING FISH STEAKS, especially meaty ones like cod steaks, ensures moistness. And while this recipe seems deceptively simple, the combination of a mild-flavored white fish and a spirited Southwestern-style salsa of roasted corn is appealing indeed. Add a salad of peppery greens, and you have a summertime meal that is both easy to prepare and stylish. It's also low in fat. Be sure not to overcook the fish.

4	8-ounce cod steaks, cut 1 inch thick	Salt and freshly ground black pepper
2	tablespoons unsalted butter, melted	Roasted Corn Salsa (page 38)
	Fresh lemon juice	

1. Preheat the oven to 450°F. Butter a shallow baking dish large enough to hold the cod in a single layer.

2. Arrange the cod in the dish, pour the butter over it, turning to coat both sides, and season with lemon juice and salt and pepper to taste. Roast for 8 to 12 minutes, or until the fish just flakes when tested with a fork.

3. Transfer the steaks to heated dinner plates, top with the salsa and serve immediately.

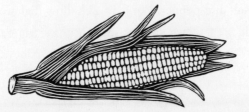

Roasted Curried Bluefish Fillets

Serves 4

Preparation time: 50 minutes (includes toasting the cumin, making the marinade and marinating the fish) ❖ *Cooking time: 15 minutes*

THE BEST BLUEFISH is the freshest—just caught, if possible. Curry-flavored yogurt marinade tames the assertive nature of this dark-fleshed, seasonal fish. Rice pilaf would make a fitting accompaniment, with a medley of roasted vegetables as a first course.

2 tablespoons vegetable oil	1 tablespoon fresh lemon juice
½ cup minced onion	Salt and freshly ground black pepper
1 large garlic clove, minced	4 8-ounce bluefish fillets, skinned
1 tablespoon curry powder, or to taste	1½ cups plain dry bread crumbs
1 cup low-fat plain yogurt	2 tablespoons minced fresh cilantro
1 teaspoon cumin seeds, toasted and ground (see page 34)	4 tablespoons (½ stick) unsalted butter, melted

1. In a small skillet, heat the oil over medium heat until hot. Add the onion and garlic and cook, stirring, for 2 to 3 minutes, or until the onion is softened. Add the curry powder and cook over low heat, stirring, for 2 minutes. Transfer to a bowl and stir in the yogurt, cumin, lemon juice and salt and pepper to taste.

2. Season the bluefish with salt and pepper. Put it in a shallow dish and pour the marinade over it, turning the fillets to coat both sides. Cover and marinate in the refrigerator for 30 minutes.

3. Preheat the oven to 500°F. Lightly oil a shallow baking dish large enough to hold the fillets in a single layer.

4. On a large plate, combine the bread crumbs, cilantro and salt and pepper to taste. Remove the fillets from the marinade, letting the excess drip off, then dredge in the seasoned crumbs, coating completely. Arrange in the baking dish and drizzle with the butter. Roast for 12 to 15 minutes, or until the fillets just flake when tested with a fork. Serve immediately.

Roasted Halibut Steaks *with* Herbed Potato Crust

Serves 4

Preparation time: 15 minutes ❖ *Cooking time: 13 minutes*

NOBODY NEEDS TO BE REMINDED of how well suited fish and potatoes are to each other. We've kept the basic combination but added a twist: Instead of serving potatoes as an accompaniment, we've grated them, mixed them with herbs and patted them onto halibut steaks. The herbed coating keeps the fish moist as it crisps.

Roasted Tomatoes Provençale (page 196) on a bed of steamed or quickly sautéed baby spinach would make just the right vegetable side dish.

4	8-ounce halibut steaks, cut 1 inch thick	3	tablespoons snipped fresh chives or minced fresh parsley, or a combination
⅓	cup Dijon mustard		Salt and freshly ground black pepper
2	Idaho potatoes, peeled and finely grated	3	tablespoons olive oil
2	teaspoons minced fresh rosemary, or 1 teaspoon dried, crumbled		
2	teaspoons minced fresh thyme, or 1 teaspoon dried, crumbled		

1. Preheat the oven to 450°F.

2. Brush both sides of the halibut steaks with the mustard. Set aside.

3. With your hands, squeeze out as much moisture as possible from the grated potatoes. In a bowl, combine the grated potatoes with all the herbs and salt and pepper to taste. Pat the potato mixture onto both sides of the fish steaks, pressing it so it adheres.

4. In a large ovenproof skillet, heat the oil over medium-high heat until hot. Add the fish and cook for 2 to 3 minutes, or until golden brown on the bottom. Turn the fish, then transfer the skillet to the oven. Roast for 10 minutes, or until the fish just flakes when tested with a fork. Serve immediately.

Roasted Red Snapper Fillets *with* Tomatoes, Clams *and* Mussels

Serves 4
Preparation time: 30 minutes
Cooking time: 45 minutes (includes making the sauce)

I F YOU ARE ACCUSTOMED to broiled red snapper, you will immediately note the difference in fillets that have been roasted. Roasting at very high heat (500°F) for a comparatively short time (10 minutes maximum) results in fillets that remain juicy.

A sauce made with the ingredients associated with bouillabaisse—tomatoes, garlic, fennel and clams—ensures moistness and a Mediterranean flavor. Add additional clams and mussels, if you like, and be sure to have a fresh baguette on hand to tuck into the sauce.

2 tablespoons olive oil	1½ teaspoons minced fresh thyme, or ½ teaspoon dried, crumbled
1 medium-large onion, minced	¼ teaspoon fennel seeds, crushed
½ cup minced fennel bulb	1 tablespoon tomato paste
1 16-ounce can tomatoes, drained and chopped	Salt and freshly ground black pepper
1 tablespoon minced garlic	4 cherrystone clams, scrubbed
2 cups homemade or canned chicken stock	8 mussels, scrubbed and debearded
⅓ cup minced fresh parsley	4 6-ounce red snapper fillets
	2 tablespoons unsalted butter, melted

1. In a large pot, heat the oil over medium heat until hot. Cook the onion and minced fennel, stirring occasionally, for 3 minutes, or until softened. Add the tomatoes and garlic and cook, stirring, for 2 minutes, or until the garlic is fragrant. Add the stock, 3 tablespoons of the parsley, the thyme, fennel seeds, tomato paste and salt and pepper to taste. Bring to a boil, reduce the heat to low and simmer, stirring occasionally, for 20 minutes.

2. Add the clams and mussels, cover, and cook over medium-high heat, shaking the pan occasionally, until the shellfish have opened, about 5 minutes. With a slotted spoon, transfer the clams and mussels to a bowl. Cover and keep warm.

3. Reduce the tomato mixture over medium-high heat until thickened to a saucelike consistency, 3 to 5 minutes. Stir in the remaining parsley. Remove from the heat, cover and keep warm.

4. Meanwhile, preheat the oven to 500°F. Butter a baking dish large enough to hold the fillets in a single layer.

5. Arrange the fillets, skin side down, in the pan, season with salt and pepper to taste and drizzle with the melted butter. Roast for 8 to 10 minutes, or until firm to the touch. Carefully transfer the fillets to a heated platter, arrange the reserved shellfish around the rim, top the fillets with the sauce and serve.

Roasted Red Snapper Greek Style

Serves 4

Preparation time: 15 minutes ❖ *Cooking time: 25 minutes*

A MAGNIFICENT WHOLE FISH would be ideal for this recipe. But because a 4-to-4½-pound red snapper is hard to find, we call for two smaller fish—less dramatic, but no less good to eat.

Quality ingredients determine the success of a dish as unadorned as this. Maximize the Greek flavors: Use Greek olive oil, begin with a Greek salad and serve minted orzo and Roasted Zucchini with Red Onion (page 199) as accompaniments. Roasted Prune Plums with Almond Topping (page 232) makes a tasty dessert.

2	1½-to-2-pound red snappers, cleaned, heads and tails left on, rinsed and patted dry		Salt and freshly ground black pepper
2	garlic cloves	3	tablespoons olive oil
2	teaspoons minced fresh oregano, or 1 teaspoon dried, crumbled		Lemon wedges, for garnish
		1	tablespoon minced fresh parsley, for garnish

1. Preheat the oven to 450°F. Lightly oil a baking dish large enough the hold the fish without crowding.

2. Rub the cavities of the fish with the garlic and season with the oregano and salt and pepper to taste. Arrange the fish in the baking dish and drizzle with the oil. Roast for 10 minutes, basting with the pan juices. Continue to roast, basting, for 10 to 15 minutes longer, or until the fish just flakes when tested with a fork.

3. With a metal spatula, transfer the fish to a platter. Garnish with the lemon wedges and parsley and serve.

Roasted Salmon Steaks *with* Hoisin Glaze

Serves 4

Preparation time: 40 minutes (includes marinating the salmon)

Cooking time: 10 minutes

REMEMBER THIS RECIPE when you need a simple but fabulous dish at the last minute. Hoisin sauce, a Chinese staple made of soybeans, garlic and spices, quickly infuses the salmon with flavor. The roasting temperature of 500°F keeps cooking time to a minimum.

For contrasting texture and color, serve over a grated daikon salad.

For the hoisin glaze
- 1 tablespoon minced fresh ginger
- 2 large garlic cloves, minced
- ⅓ cup rice vinegar
- ⅓ cup homemade or canned chicken stock
- 3 tablespoons hoisin sauce
- 1 tablespoon Asian sesame oil
- ¼ teaspoon red pepper flakes
-    Salt and freshly ground black pepper to taste

- 4 8-ounce salmon steaks, cut 1 inch thick

1. **Make the hoisin glaze:** In a shallow, nonreactive dish, combine all the glaze ingredients. Add the salmon steaks, turn to coat them with the marinade, cover and marinate in the refrigerator for 30 minutes.

2. Preheat the oven to 500°F. Lightly oil a baking dish large enough to hold the fish in a single layer.

3. Arrange the salmon steaks in the baking dish and roast, brushing occasionally with the remaining glaze, for 8 to 10 minutes, or until firm but still springy to the touch.

4. Transfer the salmon to a serving platter, pour any glaze remaining in the baking dish over the top and serve.

Roasted Sea Bass *with* Bread Stuffing

Serves 4

Preparation time: 20 minutes (includes making the stuffing) ❖ *Cooking time: 45 minutes*

As CHINESE COOKS HAVE KNOWN FOR CENTURIES, there is drama to be had when a whole fish (including the head) is brought to the dinner table. This recipe creates the same effect, but is different in one important way. Whereas the Chinese frequently deep-fry whole fish, this fish is roasted, making it virtually free of fat.

You will need the freshest sea bass. The bread stuffing is very simple—the best kind. The moist result is just right for a cool summer night. Roasted Tomatoes Provençale (page 196) can accompany the dish, along with a platter of broccoli rabe sautéed in olive oil with crispy minced garlic.

For the bread stuffing
- 2 tablespoons olive oil
- ½ cup minced shallots (3-4 large shallots)
- ¼ cup minced celery
- 2 garlic cloves, minced
- 1 cup plain dry bread crumbs
- 1 teaspoon grated lemon zest
- ¼ cup minced fresh parsley
- ½ teaspoon dried, crumbled thyme
- Salt and freshly ground black pepper

For the bass
- 1 3½-to-4-pound sea bass, cleaned, head and tail left on, rinsed and patted dry
- 1½ tablespoons olive oil
- Lemon wedges, for serving

1. Preheat the oven to 400°F. Generously oil a roasting pan large enough to hold the bass.

2. **Make the bread stuffing:** In a medium skillet, heat the 2 tablespoons oil over medium heat until hot. Cook the shallots, stirring, for 2 minutes, or until softened. Add the celery and garlic and cook for 5 minutes more, or until softened. Transfer the vegetables to a bowl and add the bread crumbs, lemon zest, parsley, thyme and salt and pepper to taste; mix well.

3. **Prepare the bass:** Season the inside of the fish with salt and pepper and loosely pack the fish with the stuffing. Close the opening of the fish with wooden toothpicks or skewers and brush the oil on both sides. Sprinkle the fish with salt and pepper to taste.

4. Place the fish in the roasting pan and roast, basting frequently with the pan juices, for 45 minutes, or until the fish just flakes when tested with a fork. Transfer the fish to a heated serving platter and garnish the platter with the lemon wedges. Remove the picks or skewers before serving.

Roasted Trout Provençale

Serves 4

Preparation time: 30 minutes (includes making the sauce) ❖ *Cooking time: 15 minutes*

THIS VEGETABLE-SAUCED TROUT sparkles with the flavors of the South of France. Couscous would make a superb accompaniment, as would parslied steamed potatoes or garlic mashed potatoes—both suited for the French theme. The sauce can be made in advance and refrigerated, leaving just 15 minutes of cooking time.

For the trout

- 4 12-ounce brook or rainbow trout, cleaned, heads and tails left on, rinsed and patted dry
  Salt and freshly ground black pepper
- 4 sprigs fresh thyme, or 1 teaspoon dried, crumbled
- 1 tablespoon extra-virgin olive oil

For the sauce

- 2 tablespoons extra-virgin olive oil
- 1 cup minced onion
- 2 garlic cloves, minced
- ⅓ cup dry white wine
- 2 cups drained, chopped canned tomatoes (two 16-ounce cans)
- 1 tablespoon tomato paste
- 1 teaspoon minced fresh thyme, or ½ teaspoon dried, crumbled
- 16 kalamata olives, pitted and coarsely chopped

- 2 tablespoons minced fresh parsley, for garnish

1. **Prepare the trout:** Preheat the oven to 450°F. Lightly oil a shallow baking dish large enough to hold the trout in a single layer.

2. Season the trout with salt and pepper to taste. Arrange a sprig of thyme in the cavity of each fish or sprinkle with dried thyme and drizzle a total of 1 tablespoon of the oil into the cavities.

3. **Make the sauce:** In a skillet, heat the oil over medium heat until hot. Add the onion and garlic and cook, stirring occasionally, for 3 to 5 minutes, or until softened. Add the wine and boil for 1 minute to reduce the sauce. Add the tomatoes, tomato paste, thyme and salt and pepper to taste. Simmer, stirring occasionally, for 10 to 15 minutes, or until the sauce is thick.

4. Spoon half of the sauce into the baking dish and arrange the trout over the sauce. Top with the remaining sauce. Roast for 10 minutes. Scatter the olives over the top and roast for 5 minutes more, or until the fish just flakes when tested with a fork. Serve garnished with the parsley.

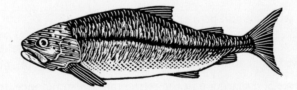

*R*oasted Tuna Teriyaki *with* Wasabi Cream Sauce

Serves 4

Preparation time: 45 minutes (includes marinating the tuna and making and chilling the sauce)
Cooking time: 5 to 10 minutes

I F YOU LIKE YOUR TUNA pink on the inside, remove the steaks from the oven after 5 minutes. If you prefer tuna that is only slightly pink, roast them longer and get a dividend: a delicious caramelization of the teriyaki marinade.

4	8-ounce tuna steaks, cut 1 inch thick	1	tablespoon honey
	Salt and freshly ground black pepper	1	tablespoon vegetable oil
3	tablespoons reduced-sodium soy sauce	2	teaspoons minced fresh ginger
2	tablespoons rice wine vinegar	1	large garlic clove, finely minced
			Wasabi Cream Sauce, for serving

1. Season the tuna steaks with salt and pepper.

2. In a shallow, nonreactive dish, combine the soy sauce, vinegar, honey, oil, ginger and garlic. Add the tuna and turn to coat. Cover and marinate in the refrigerator, turning once, for 30 minutes.

3. Preheat the oven to 500°F. Lightly oil a baking dish.

4. Remove the tuna from the marinade and place the steaks in a single layer on the baking dish. Roast for 5 minutes for rare or 10 minutes for slightly pink, or until the fish just flakes when tested with a fork.

5. Transfer the tuna to dinner plates and serve with the wasabi cream sauce.

WASABI CREAM SAUCE

Makes about 1 cup
Preparation time: 5 minutes ❖ *Cooking time: None*

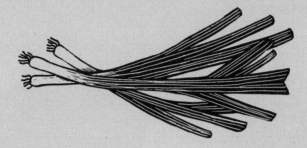

YOU PROBABLY KNOW WASABI as the lethal little mound of super-hot green paste, sometimes called Japanese horseradish, that accompanies sushi or sashimi. Wasabi powder, which can be purchased in specialty shops, is no less fiery. Increase the amount of wasabi, if you like, keeping the ratio of powder to water equal.

1   tablespoon wasabi powder
1   cup sour cream
2   tablespoons snipped scallion tops
    Salt to taste
    Fresh lemon juice to taste

In a bowl, dissolve the wasabi powder in 1 tablespoon water. Add the remaining ingredients, whisking until combined. Cover and chill for 30 minutes.

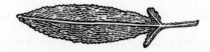

Chapter IV

Poultry

THANK HEAVEN FOR THAT GREAT SOLUTION when all else fails: dependable roast chicken, familiar but delicious, elegant enough for a Sunday dinner party, informal enough for a weekday supper.

Simple it may be, but for good cooks, there is absolutely no taking for granted *how* a chicken should be roasted. Differences of opinion abound about the best way. There are theories as to temperature, cooking time and doneness, to mention only the most obvious bones of contention. Should the bird be cooked at a consistent temperature or browned at high heat and then cooked slowly? Is a rack necessary?

We prefer to start a whole chicken roasting at an initial high heat, then reduce the heat for the greater part of the cooking time. This method, as opposed to the one that roasts the bird at a lower temperature for the duration, results in the best combination of crisp, golden skin and moist meat. The higher initial temperature sears the exterior, browning it and enhancing flavor, a process that generally takes between 20 to 25 minutes at 450°F. Then the temperature is lowered for slower, more gentle cooking, producing juicy meat. As with any whole bird, basting is essential for even browning and moistness. The proof is in the tasting: Try our Roasted Lemon Chicken (page 112) and see for yourself.

We recommend using a rack when roasting a whole bird to allow for a more even flow of heat and to prevent the skin from sticking to the bottom of the pan. You can use a standard metal V-shaped model or simply place the bird on a base of vegetables—carrots, celery and onions—to elevate it slightly. The advantage to using a vegetable "rack" is twofold: The vegetables flavor the chicken as it roasts, and they absorb its juices, becoming a superb accompaniment to the meal.

We consider our chickens to be done when the legs move easily at the joints and the juices run clear (not pinkish) when the thigh is pricked. A worthwhile investment is an instant-read thermometer. For a whole bird, insert it in the thigh, avoiding the bone, or for a breast, in the thickest part. Poultry is cooked through when the thermometer registers 165°F. Always remember to let a whole roasted chicken stand for 10 minutes before carving—longer for turkey—to allow the juices to settle into the meat. During this time, the bird continues to cook for a few minutes even though it is out of the oven—another reason to pay close attention to cooking times.

The selections in this chapter range from informal combinations, like Roasted Chicken Wings with Onions, Potatoes and Red Pepper (page 124) to sophisticated party fare, like Roasted Duck Breast with Balsamic Orange Sauce (page 132).

Poultry

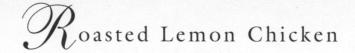

Roasted Lemon Chicken

Serves 4

Preparation time: 10 minutes ❖ *Cooking time: 1 hour*

ANYONE WHO HAS EVER eaten dried-out, overcooked chicken will particularly appreciate this delectable, juicy bird. A whole lemon contributes to the pan juices, and a generous amount of rosemary renders the dish wonderfully aromatic. It is well worth tracking down fresh rosemary for that reason alone. Rice is good with this. So is roasted broccoli or asparagus, brushed with a bit of melted butter.

For the chicken

1   3-to-3½-pound chicken,
      rinsed and patted dry
      Salt and freshly ground black pepper
1   sprig fresh rosemary, or
      1 teaspoon dried, crumbled
1   garlic clove, crushed
1   lemon, pricked in a few places
      with a sharp knife (see Tip)
1½ tablespoons olive oil

For the vegetables

1   large onion, cut into thick slices
1   small celery stalk, cut into thick slices
1   small carrot, cut into thick slices
2   teaspoons minced fresh rosemary,
      or 1 teaspoon dried, crumbled
      Salt and freshly ground black pepper
1   tablespoon olive oil

1. **Prepare the chicken:** Preheat the oven to 450°F.

2. Season the cavity of the chicken with salt and pepper to taste. Add the rosemary sprig to the cavity or sprinkle with the dried rosemary, add the garlic and lemon and truss the chicken (see Tip, page 127). Brush the skin with the oil and season with salt and pepper.

3. **Make the vegetables:** In a roasting pan, combine the onion, celery, carrot, rosemary and salt and pepper to taste. Drizzle the vegetables with the oil and toss.

4. Place the chicken on the vegetables and roast for 20 minutes, or until golden. Lower the oven temperature to 375°F and roast, basting frequently with the pan juices, for 35 to 40 minutes more, or until the juices run clear when the thigh is pricked with a fork and a meat thermometer registers 165°F. Transfer the chicken and vegetables, with the pan juices, to a platter. Let stand for 10 minutes before carving.

❖ Use a lemon that yields to a squeeze, indicating juiciness within. Also, before pricking the fruit, roll it back and forth on the countertop a few times to soften it. If possible, avoid hard, thick-skinned lemons. You want a fruit that will yield both juice and fragrance.

*B*arbecued Chicken

Serves 4; makes 1 cup barbecue sauce
Preparation time: 10 minutes (includes making the sauce) ❖ *Cooking time: 1 hour*

WE EAT BARBECUED CHICKEN OFTEN. The kids like it; it's tasty hot, at room temperature or cold; and we can have it year-round. This version is not grilled, however, but roasted. To ensure juicy, tender meat, baste the chicken first with the garlic-and-oil mixture, and then with the pan juices, and finally, brush it with the chili barbecue sauce. Serve with fresh-baked corn bread and slaw or old-fashioned potato salad, in keeping with the Southern tradition.

The barbecue sauce is very easy to put together—one bowl, no cooking. And it stores well. Make a double batch and keep it, tightly covered, in the refrigerator for up to one week.

For the barbecue sauce
- ⅓ cup chili sauce
- ¼ cup ketchup
- ¼ cup cider vinegar
- 1 tablespoon dark brown sugar
- 1 tablespoon Worcestershire sauce
- 1 tablespoon Dijon mustard
- ½ teaspoon Tabasco, or to taste

For the chicken
- 3 tablespoons olive oil
- 3 garlic cloves, minced
- ½ teaspoon dried, crumbled rosemary
- ½ teaspoon dried, crumbled thyme
- Salt and freshly ground black pepper
- 1 3-to-3½-pound chicken, rinsed and patted dry, halved and backbone removed (see Tip)

1. **Make the barbecue sauce:** In a bowl, combine all the sauce ingredients.

2. **Prepare the chicken:** Preheat the oven to 450°F.

3. In a small bowl, combine the oil, garlic, herbs and salt and pepper to taste; brush the chicken all over with the mixture. Place the chicken, skin side up, on a rack in a roasting pan and roast for 20 minutes, or until the skin is golden brown. Turn, baste with the pan juices, and roast for 20 minutes more. Turn skin side up, brush with the barbecue sauce, and roast for 10 minutes more, basting with the remaining sauce, until the juices run clear when the thigh is pricked with a fork. Transfer the chicken to a heated platter and serve.

❖ **To remove the backbone, cut along one side with a heavy knife or kitchen shears. Repeat on the other side. Lift the backbone out and discard it. Pull out the breast bone, the dark-colored V-shaped cartilage in front of the wishbone, and discard it too.**

Roasted Chicken Breasts *with* Eggplant *and* Zucchini *in* Fennel-Tomato Sauce

Serves 4

Preparation time: 20 minutes ❖ *Cooking time: 30 minutes (includes making the sauce)*

IF YOU ARE LOOKING FOR NEW THINGS to do with chicken—and who isn't?—try this. It is a dandy dish for fall. It's worth noting that the fennel-tomato sauce takes longer to cook than the chicken and vegetables. If you make it ahead of time, you can have dinner on the table in roughly 15 minutes. We like this served over spinach pasta.

For the fennel-tomato sauce

- 2 tablespoons olive oil
- 1 cup minced onion
- ½ cup minced fennel bulb
- 3 garlic cloves, minced
- 1 28-ounce can crushed tomatoes in puree
- 1 teaspoon fennel seeds, crushed
- ½ teaspoon dried, crumbled rosemary
- 1 bay leaf
- 1 cup homemade or canned chicken stock
  Salt and freshly ground black pepper

For the chicken and vegetables

- 2 whole chicken breasts, halved
- 1 medium-to-small eggplant (about 8 ounces), trimmed and cut into quarters
- 2 small zucchini, trimmed and halved lengthwise
- 1 red bell pepper, cored, seeded and cut into 1-inch pieces
- ¼ cup olive oil
- 1 teaspoon dried, crumbled rosemary

- 2 tablespoons minced fresh parsley, for garnish

1. **Make the fennel-tomato sauce:** In a large saucepan, heat the oil over medium heat until hot. Cook the onion and minced fennel, stirring occasionally, for 5 minutes, or until softened. Add the garlic and cook, stirring, for 1 minute more. Add the tomatoes, fennel seeds, rosemary, bay leaf, stock and salt and pepper to taste. Simmer, stirring occasionally, for 20 minutes. Remove from the heat, fish out the bay leaf, cover and keep warm while the chicken and vegetables roast. (The sauce may be prepared 1 day in advance and refrigerated.)

2. **Meanwhile, prepare the chicken and vegetables:** Preheat the oven to 500°F.

3. In a large roasting pan, arrange the chicken, eggplant, zucchini and bell pepper in a single layer. Drizzle with the oil, sprinkle with the rosemary and season with salt and pepper to taste. Roast, turning the chicken and vegetables once or twice, for 15 to 20 minutes, or until the juices run clear when the breasts are pricked with a fork and the vegetables are tender. Transfer to a serving platter, nap with the sauce and garnish with the parsley.

Roasted Citrus Chicken Breasts

with Sweet-*and*-Sour Sauce

Serves 6
Preparation time: 2 hours 20 minutes (includes marinating the chicken)
Cooking time: 20 minutes

THESE CHICKEN BREASTS are elegant enough to serve to company, and they roast in just 20 minutes. Serve with quinoa or couscous—or with good bread to soak up the light sauce—and with a double recipe of Roasted Zucchini with Red Onion (page 199). For dessert, bring out Roasted Gingered Nectarines with Pecan Topping (page 234).

For the citrus marinade
½ cup minced shallots
(3-4 large shallots)
2 teaspoons grated orange zest
⅓ cup fresh orange juice
3 tablespoons fresh lemon juice
3 tablespoons reduced-sodium soy sauce
3 tablespoons rice vinegar
2 tablespoons honey
1 tablespoon minced fresh ginger
1 tablespoon Dijon mustard
3 garlic cloves, minced
Salt to taste
Red pepper flakes to taste

For the chicken
3 whole chicken breasts, halved
2 tablespoons vegetable oil
1 tablespoon Asian sesame oil
2 cups homemade or canned beef stock
1½ tablespoons arrowroot
3 tablespoons fresh orange juice
2 teaspoons Dijon mustard
2 teaspoons honey
Salt and freshly ground black pepper

2 tablespoons minced fresh cilantro,
for garnish

1. **Make the marinade:** In a shallow, nonreactive dish, combine all the marinade ingredients. Add the chicken, cover and marinate in the refrigerator, turning once or twice, for at least 2 hours, or overnight.

2. **Prepare the chicken:** Preheat the oven to 500°F.

3. Remove the chicken from the marinade, pat it dry and arrange it on a rack in a shallow roasting pan. Reserve the marinade.

4. In a small bowl, combine the oils and brush on the chicken. Roast, turning once, for 15 to 20 minutes, or until the juices run clear when the breasts are pricked with a fork. Transfer to a platter.

5. While the chicken is roasting, combine the reserved marinade with the stock in a small saucepan and boil over medium-high heat to reduce to 1½ cups. In a small bowl, combine the arrowroot with the orange juice and add it to the simmering stock mixture, whisking until lightly thickened, 1 to 2 minutes. Stir in the mustard, honey and salt and pepper to taste.

6. Nap the chicken with some sauce and garnish with the cilantro. Serve the remaining sauce separately.

*B*uttermilk-Marinated Parmesan-Crumbed Chicken Legs

Serves 6

Preparation time: 2 hours 20 minutes (includes marinating the chicken)

Cooking time: 40 minutes

*B*UTTERMILK TENDERIZES THE CHICKEN, and roasting crisps the crumb coating. These chicken legs are great for picnics and simple suppers. You can start marinating the pieces the night before. If you use breasts, shorten the cooking time accordingly.

For the buttermilk marinade

- 1½ cups buttermilk
- 1 tablespoon fresh lemon juice
- 1 tablespoon Dijon mustard
- 1 tablespoon minced garlic
- ½ teaspoon salt
- ¼ teaspoon cayenne pepper

For the chicken

- 3 pounds chicken legs, cut into drumsticks and thighs, skinned
- 1½ cups plain dry bread crumbs
- ⅔ cup freshly grated Parmesan
  Salt and freshly ground black pepper
- 8 tablespoons (1 stick) unsalted butter, melted, for drizzling

1. **Make the buttermilk marinade:** In a shallow dish, combine all the marinade ingredients. Add the chicken pieces, turn to coat, cover and marinate in the refrigerator for at least 2 hours, or overnight.

2. **Prepare the chicken:** Preheat the oven to 400°F. Lightly oil 2 large baking sheets.

3. Remove the chicken from the marinade and let the excess marinade drain off. In a shallow dish, combine the bread crumbs, Parmesan and salt and pepper to taste. Dredge each chicken piece in the crumb mixture and place on the baking sheet, taking care not to let the pieces touch so they will become crisp. Drizzle the butter over the chicken and roast for 40 minutes, or until the juices run clear when the thighs are pricked with a fork. Serve hot or at room temperature.

*T*andoori Chicken Legs

Serves 4 to 6
Preparation time: 2 hours 20 minutes (includes marinating the chicken)
Cooking time: 25 minutes

THIS CHICKEN HAS ALL THE FLAVOR of the famous Indian preparation, but it is easier—and you don't need a tandoor oven. Because the traditional tandoori coloring paste with its artificial color is not used in the marinade, the chicken emerges a natural brown rather than brilliant red. It will be spicy even when made with only one jalapeño. Proceed with caution if you are using two chilies, and serve a simple rice pilaf as an accompaniment to help tame the blaze.

A last word of caution: Because the oven is set at 500°F, you should start checking the chicken for doneness after 20 minutes.

For the marinade
1   tablespoon paprika
2   teaspoons cumin seeds, toasted
     and ground (see Tip, page 34)
1   teaspoon ground cardamom
½   teaspoon cayenne pepper
¼   teaspoon ground cloves
3   garlic cloves, mashed to a paste
1-2 jalapeños, seeded, if desired,
     and minced
1   tablespoon minced fresh ginger
½   cup low-fat plain yogurt
2   tablespoons fresh lemon juice
     Salt and freshly ground black pepper

For the chicken
2   pounds chicken legs, skinned
3-4 tablespoons ghee (Indian clarified
     butter, available at Indian markets)
     or unsalted butter, melted

     Lemon wedges and fresh cilantro
       sprigs, for garnish

1. **Make the marinade:** In a blender or food processor, puree the paprika, cumin, cardamom, cayenne, cloves, garlic, jalapeños, ginger, yogurt, lemon juice and salt and pepper to taste until the marinade is smooth.

2. **Prepare the chicken:** With a sharp knife, make ½-inch diagonal slashes all over the chicken legs. Rub the marinade into the chicken, especially into the slits, cover and marinate in the refrigerator for at least 2 hours, or overnight, turning two or three times.

3. Preheat the oven to 500°F.

4. Remove the chicken from the marinade, allowing the excess to drip off, and arrange the pieces on a rack in a roasting pan. Discard the marinade. Brush the pieces with the ghee or butter and roast for 20 to 25 minutes, or until the juices run clear when the thighs are pricked with a fork.

5. Transfer the chicken to a serving platter and garnish with the lemon wedges and cilantro sprigs.

Roasted Chicken Wings *with* Onions, Potatoes *and* Red Pepper

Serves 4

Preparation time: 20 minutes ❖ *Cooking time: 35 minutes*

HERE IS A RECIPE FOR ROASTED WINGS that includes a healthy serving of vegetables. Be sure to eat the garlic cloves; they're softened and mellowed by roasting and are particularly tasty. For aesthetic reasons, we prefer to remove the wing tips before cooking. (The tip is the pointed, narrow joint on the end that has no meat.) To remove it, simply cut through the joint with a heavy knife. (Reserve the wing tips in the freezer for making chicken stock.)

This one-dish dinner needs little more than a crisp green salad and a loaf of crusty bread as accompaniments, making it an easy weeknight meal.

2½	pounds chicken wings, tips removed	1	medium-to-large red bell pepper, cored, seeded and cut into 1-inch pieces
	Salt and freshly ground black pepper		
2-3	tablespoons olive oil	4	whole garlic cloves
4	medium Idaho potatoes, peeled and cut into eighths	2	teaspoons minced fresh rosemary, or 1 teaspoon dried, crumbled
2	medium-to-large onions, peeled and cut into eighths	1	cup homemade or canned chicken stock
		2	tablespoons minced fresh parsley

1. Preheat the oven to 450°F.

2. Season the wings with salt and pepper and brush them with some of the oil.

3. In a large bowl, combine the potatoes, onions, bell pepper, garlic, rosemary and salt and pepper to taste. Add just enough of the remaining oil to coat the vegetables and toss.

4. Transfer the vegetables to a roasting pan and top with the wings. Roast, turning occasionally, for 25 to 30 minutes, or until the juices run clear when the wings are pricked with a fork and the vegetables are fork-tender. Transfer the wings to a serving platter. With a slotted spoon, transfer the vegetables to the platter.

5. Pour off the fat from the roasting pan and add the stock. Bring to a boil, scraping up the brown bits on the bottom of the pan. Reduce the heat to low and simmer for 5 minutes to blend the flavors. Strain the pan gravy over the chicken and vegetables and sprinkle with the parsley.

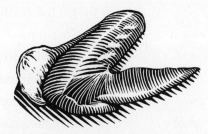

Roasted Cornish Game Hens *with* Gingered Orange Glaze

Serves 4
Preparation time: 2 hours 20 minutes (includes marinating the hens)
Cooking time: 40 minutes

THIS SIMPLE RECIPE has no seasonal limitations: It is as good served straight from the oven on a cold winter night as it is presented at room temperature on a summer evening. The higher heat of the initial roasting and repeated basting guarantee burnished, succulent little birds.

For the marinade

- 2 teaspoons grated orange zest
- 1 teaspoon grated lemon zest
- 1 cup fresh orange juice
- ¼ cup fresh lemon juice
- ⅓ cup reduced-sodium soy sauce
- 2 tablespoons minced fresh ginger
- 1 tablespoon minced garlic
  Salt and freshly ground black pepper

For the hens

- 4 1-pound Cornish game hens, rinsed and patted dry
- 3 tablespoons unsalted butter, softened
- ½ cup honey
- 3 tablespoons balsamic vinegar
- 3 tablespoons Dijon mustard

1. **Make the marinade:** In a small bowl, combine the orange and lemon zests, the orange and lemon juices, the soy sauce, ginger, garlic and salt and pepper to taste. Place the hens in a nonreactive baking dish. Spoon some of the marinade into the cavity of each hen, then spoon the remaining marinade over them. Cover and marinate in the refrigerator, turning once, for at least 2 hours, or overnight.

2. **Prepare the hens:** Preheat the oven to 425°F.

3. Remove the hens from the marinade and pat dry, reserving the marinade. Truss the hens (see Tip) and brush them with the butter. Place them on a rack in a roasting pan and roast, basting occasionally with the pan juices, for 20 minutes.

4. Meanwhile, pour the marinade into a small nonreactive saucepan. Stir in the honey, vinegar and mustard and simmer over medium heat, stirring occasionally, until thick enough to coat a spoon.

5. Reduce the oven temperature to 375°F. Spoon the glaze over the hens and roast, basting frequently, for 20 minutes more, or until the juices run clear when the thighs are pricked with a fork and a meat thermometer registers 165°F. Let stand for 10 minutes and remove the strings from the hens before serving. They can be served hot, at room temperature or chilled.

❖ Trussing not only produces a better-looking finished bird but a more evenly cooked one. The simplest way to truss is to tie the ends of the drumsticks together with kitchen string, overlapping them slightly.

For a more elaborate presentation, place the bird breast side up on a work surface. Cut a long piece of kitchen string and position the middle of it under the tail of the chicken. Bring the strings up to cross over the top of the tail. Extend each string, wrapping it around the tip of each drumstick, then cross the strings again, pulling the drumsticks together to close the tail opening in a figure 8. (Do not pull so hard on the strings that the skin splits.) Extend each string along the lower portion of each side of the breast, looping it through the angle made by the joint of the wings and extend it around the neck opening. Carefully turn the chicken over, breast side down. Double-knot the string and trim the ends. Reposition the bird breast side up.

Roasted Herb-Stuffed Cornish Game Hens

with Lemon Butter

Serves 4
Preparation time: 20 minutes ❖ *Cooking time: 1 hour*

THERE IS SOMETHING SPECIAL about Cornish game hens—mostly because they are a pleasant change from chicken and because of their diminutive size. These little birds are fragrant with fresh herbs and lemon. Add steamed rice and asparagus, and you have a lovely springtime menu.

You can also serve these hens at room temperature. Leftovers make superb sandwiches on sourdough bread. Use the herb mixture to dress up chicken as well.

2	1½-pound Cornish game hens, split, rinsed and patted dry	2	tablespoons minced fresh parsley
1	tablespoon olive oil	1	tablespoon minced fresh rosemary, or 1 teaspoon dried, crumbled
½	cup minced shallots (3-4 large shallots)	4	teaspoons grated lemon zest
2	tablespoons minced fresh tarragon, or 1 teaspoon dried, crumbled	2	teaspoons finely minced garlic
			Salt and freshly ground black pepper
2	tablespoons snipped fresh chives or scallion tops	2	tablespoons unsalted butter, softened
		1	tablespoon fresh lemon juice

1. Preheat the oven to 400°F.

2. Loosen the breast skin of each hen by gently slipping your fingers between the skin and the flesh, being careful not to tear the skin.

3. In a small saucepan, heat the oil over medium heat until hot. Add the shallots and cook, stirring, for 3 minutes, or until softened. Transfer the shallots to a bowl and add the tarragon, chives or scallions, parsley, rosemary, 2 teaspoons of the lemon zest, the garlic and salt and pepper to taste; stir until well combined. Pat the shallot mixture under the breast skin of each hen, smoothing it so that it covers the breast meat evenly.

4. Arrange the hens in a roasting pan. In a small bowl, combine the remaining 2 teaspoons lemon zest, the butter and lemon juice and smear it over the hens. Sprinkle the hens with salt and pepper to taste.

5. Roast the hens, basting frequently with the pan juices, for 45 to 60 minutes, or until the juices run clear when the thighs are pricked with a fork and a meat thermometer registers 165°F. Transfer the hens to a heated serving platter and let stand for 10 minutes. Remove the strings from the hens before serving.

Maple-Glazed Roasted Duckling
with McIntosh Apples

Serves 4

Preparation time: 15 minutes ❖ *Cooking time: 2¼ hours*

NOT TOO MANY YEARS AGO, it was all the rage to serve rare duck. Lots of people, though, never acquired the taste for pink duck meat. This recipe is tailor-made for them. The bird begins roasting at a very high heat, ideal for rendering most of the fat. Then the heat is lowered and the duck slow-roasts to a well-cooked but still juicy tenderness.

For the glaze, use only pure maple syrup and fresh apples, meaning those picked that season. Fresh fall apples will hold their shape better during cooking than stored ones. Serve with roasted potatoes.

For the duck

1	4½-to-5-pound duckling, rinsed and patted dry, as much of the fat removed as possible
1	small onion, quartered
1	small celery stalk, quartered
3	garlic cloves
½	teaspoon dried, crumbled savory
½	teaspoon dried, crumbled sage
	Salt and freshly ground black pepper

For the glaze

⅓	cup pure maple syrup
1½	tablespoons red wine vinegar
1	tablespoon fresh lemon juice
1	tablespoon reduced-sodium soy sauce
1	tablespoon unsalted butter
2	teaspoons Dijon mustard
1	pound McIntosh apples (about 3 large), peeled, cored and quartered

1. **Prepare the duck:** Preheat the oven to 450°F.

2. Pat the duck dry with paper towels and prick it all over with the tip of a small sharp knife. Fill the cavity with the onion, celery, garlic and herbs and season with salt and pepper to taste. Place on a rack in a roasting pan and roast for 30 minutes. Reduce the oven temperature to 300°F and roast for 1¼ hours more. Drain the fat from the pan and let the duck cool until it can be handled; leave the oven on.

3. **Meanwhile, make the glaze:** In a small, nonreactive saucepan, combine all the glaze ingredients, bring to a boil and simmer for 2 minutes. Remove from the heat and set aside.

4. Increase the oven temperature to 425°F. Quarter the duck. Arrange the pieces in a baking pan, skin side up. Surround the pieces with the apples. Spoon the glaze over the duck and apples and roast, basting frequently, for 30 minutes more, or until the apples are tender and the duck is glazed. Transfer the duck and apples to a heated platter, nap with the pan juices and serve.

*R*oasted Duck Breast

with Balsamic Orange Sauce

Serves 4

Preparation time: 15 minutes ❖ *Cooking time: 30 minutes (includes making the sauce)*

ROASTING A WHOLE DUCK can be something of an undertaking because of the need to remove as much of the fat as possible—and there is always a lot of it. Roasting just the breasts is quicker and easier. (Duck breasts are available in some supermarkets and in specialty food shops.)

This is an elegant recipe, featuring the tried-and-true combination of duck and orange. The citrus provides a brisk counterpoint to the richness of the duck. The sauce, which is almost entirely fat free, can be made several hours in advance.

Serve with wild rice and a green winter vegetable like broccoli florets. A platter of Roasted Scallions (page 190) would be tasty too. One caveat: If rare duck meat, meaning deep pink, is not to your liking, increase the roasting time, but keep checking for doneness, as the breasts will continue to cook even after they are removed from the oven.

For the balsamic orange sauce

- 3   tablespoons sugar
- ¼   cup balsamic vinegar
- 1½ cups homemade or canned beef stock
- 2   teaspoons tomato paste
- 1½ teaspoons grated orange zest
- ½   teaspoon dried, crumbled thyme
- 1   bay leaf
    Pinch of ground cloves

Salt and freshly ground black pepper
- 1½ teaspoons arrowroot or cornstarch
- 2   tablespoons orange-flavored liqueur
    or fresh orange juice

- 4   7-to-8-ounce boneless duck
    breast halves

1. Preheat the oven to 500°F.

2. **Make the balsamic orange sauce:** In a medium, heavy saucepan, dissolve the sugar in the vinegar over low heat, stirring. Bring to a boil over medium-high heat, stirring, until the mixture is reduced and syrupy. Add the stock, tomato paste, orange zest, thyme, bay leaf, cloves and salt and pepper to taste and simmer, stirring occasionally, for 15 minutes.

3. In a small bowl, stir the arrowroot or cornstarch into the liqueur or orange juice, and stir it into the simmering stock mixture. Continue stirring until lightly thickened. Remove the bay leaf and adjust the seasonings, adding salt and pepper to taste if necessary. Keep warm, covered with a buttered round of waxed paper.

4. Remove as much excess fat as possible from the duck breasts and prick them all over with the tip of a small sharp knife.

5. Heat an ovenproof skillet over medium-high heat until hot. Add the duck breasts, skin side down, and sear for 3 minutes, or until the skin is golden brown. Turn the breasts skin side up and place the skillet in the oven. Roast for 8 minutes for rare meat.

6. Transfer the duck breasts to a plate and let them rest for 5 minutes. Cut each breast into diagonal slices, arrange on serving plates and nap with the warm balsamic orange sauce.

$\mathcal{R}$oasted Turkey Breast *with* Hazelnut *and* Wild Rice Stuffing

Serves 6 to 8
Preparation time: 1 hour 20 minutes (does not include cooking the wild rice or preparing the nuts)
Cooking time: 2¼ hours (includes making the gravy)

ROASTING A WHOLE TURKEY is not always convenient and can raise the specter of too many leftovers. The turkey breast is an ideal alternative. This one comes with a flavorful wild rice stuffing, studded with hazelnuts.

We start the turkey off at a high temperature to give the skin a glow, then reduce the heat to a more gentle temperature, resulting in very succulent meat. Roasted Pearl Onion and Raisin Compote (page 140) makes the perfect condiment.

For the stuffing

4   tablespoons (½ stick) unsalted butter

1½   cups minced onions

1   cup minced celery

4   garlic cloves, minced
    Salt and freshly ground black pepper

3   cups cooked wild rice
    (see Tips, page 136)

1   cup toasted, skinned hazelnuts
    (filberts), coarsely chopped
    (see Tips, page 136)

⅓   cup minced fresh parsley

1   tablespoon minced fresh sage,
    or 1½ teaspoons dried, crumbled

1   tablespoon minced fresh thyme,
    or 1 teaspoon dried, crumbled

½   cup homemade turkey stock
    or canned chicken stock

For the turkey

- 1 5-to-6-pound turkey breast
- 2 tablespoons unsalted butter, softened
  Salt and freshly ground black pepper
- 1½ teaspoons minced fresh sage,
  or ½ teaspoon dried, crumbled
- 1½ teaspoons minced fresh thyme,
  or ½ teaspoon dried, crumbled
- 1 large onion, halved
- 1 celery stalk, cut into thick slices
- 1 carrot, cut into thick slices

For the gravy

- ½ cup dry white wine
- 3 cups homemade turkey stock
  or canned chicken stock
  Worcestershire sauce
- 3 tablespoons flour
  Salt and freshly ground black pepper

1. **Make the stuffing:** In a large saucepan, melt the butter over medium heat. Add the onions, celery, garlic and salt and pepper to taste and cook, stirring, for 5 minutes, or until the vegetables are softened. Transfer to a large bowl and let cool, then add the remaining stuffing ingredients and combine well.

2. **Prepare the turkey:** Preheat the oven to 450°F.

3. Fill the neck cavity of the turkey breast with some of the stuffing and fasten it closed with a skewer. Rub the turkey skin with the butter and season with salt and pepper. Sprinkle the underside of the breast with the sage, thyme and salt and pepper. Spoon the remaining stuffing into a buttered baking dish and cover with foil.

4. Arrange the turkey on a rack in a roasting pan. Add the onion, celery and carrot to the pan and season with salt and pepper. Roast for 20 minutes, or until the turkey skin is browned. Reduce the oven temperature to 350°F and roast for 1½ hours more, or until the juices run clear and a meat thermometer registers 165°F. Transfer the turkey breast to a platter and cover loosely with foil.

5. Meanwhile, during the last 40 minutes of the roasting time, bake the reserved stuffing, covered with foil, for 30 minutes, or until completely heated through. Uncover and bake for 10 minutes more, or until the surface is golden.

6. **Make the gravy:** Pour off the fat from the roasting pan. Add the wine and bring to a boil, scraping up all the brown bits, and boil over high heat until the pan juices are reduced by half. Stir in the stock and Worcestershire sauce to taste, reduce the heat to low and simmer for 5 minutes. In a small bowl, whisk the flour with 3 tablespoons cold water until smooth. Stir the flour mixture into the simmering stock mixture and simmer, stirring occasionally, until lightly thickened. Season with salt and pepper to taste and strain into a sauceboat.

7. Carve the breast into slices and serve with the gravy.

❖ You will need roughly 1 cup wild rice to make 3 cups cooked. Follow the directions on the package and cook until the grains are just tender. Let cool completely before incorporating into the stuffing.

❖ To toast and skin the hazelnuts: Toast the nuts on a baking sheet in a preheated 350°F oven for 10 minutes, or until the skins loosen. While the nuts are still hot, wrap them in a clean kitchen towel. Let stand for 1 to 2 minutes, then rub the nuts against each other in the towel, which will remove most, but not all, of the skins.

Roasted Turkey *with* Herbed Sausage *and* Pecan Stuffing

Serves 8

Preparation time: 1 hour

Cooking time: 4 hours 20 minutes (includes making the stuffing and gravy)

HERE IS OUR THANKSGIVING TURKEY, which, due to popular demand, has been known to grace the Christmas table as well. The stuffing is festive, filled with meat, nuts and fresh herbs. Luckily for the cook, it can be made a day in advance and refrigerated separately.

There is no substitute for basting to keep the meat moist as it slow-roasts. Baste . . . baste . . . and then baste some more. A bulb baster, the kind our mothers used, makes it easy. And you might want to invest in a fat separator to make a first-class gravy, another essential part of a great holiday meal. They are available in cookware stores and cost about six dollars.

For the stuffing

1   pound sweet Italian sausage, removed from casings

6   tablespoons (¾ stick) unsalted butter

3   cups finely chopped onions

2   cups finely chopped celery

4   garlic cloves, minced

5   cups bread cubes, toasted

1½   cups chopped pecans, toasted (see Tip, page 139)

½   cup minced fresh parsley

1   tablespoon minced fresh thyme, or 1½ teaspoons dried, crumbled

1   tablespoon minced fresh sage, or 2 teaspoons dried, crumbled

½-1   cup homemade turkey stock or canned chicken stock

For the turkey

1 12-to-14-pound turkey, rinsed
   and patted dry
   Salt and freshly ground black pepper
6 tablespoons (¾ stick) unsalted
   butter, softened

For the gravy

¼ cup flour
3 cups homemade turkey stock or
   canned chicken stock, heated
2 tablespoons tomato paste
1 bay leaf
1 teaspoon dried, crumbled thyme
1 teaspoon dried, crumbled sage
   Worcestershire sauce

1. **Make the stuffing:** In a large, deep skillet, cook the sausage over medium heat, stirring, for 3 to 5 minutes, or until no longer pink. With a slotted spoon, transfer it to a large bowl. Discard the fat in the skillet. Melt the butter in the skillet over medium heat. Add the onions, celery and garlic and cook, covered, over medium-low heat, stirring occasionally, for 5 to 7 minutes, or until soft. Scrape the vegetables into the bowl with the sausage and stir well. Add the remaining stuffing ingredients except the stock to the bowl and toss to combine well. Add enough stock to moisten the stuffing slightly. (The stuffing may be made 1 day in advance; cover and store in the refrigerator.)

2. **Prepare the turkey:** Preheat the oven to 450°F.

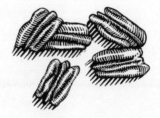

3. Season the cavity of the turkey with salt and pepper. Stuff the neck cavity loosely with some of the stuffing, fold the neck skin under the bird and fasten with a skewer. Loosely stuff the body cavity. Spoon the remaining stuffing into a buttered baking dish, cover with foil and refrigerate.

4. With strong butcher's twine, truss the turkey (see Tip, page 127), rub it with the butter and season with salt and pepper. Place the turkey on a rack in a roasting pan and roast for 30 minutes. Reduce the oven temperature to 325°F and continue roasting, basting frequently with the pan juices, for 2⅓ to 3 hours, or until the juices run clear when the thigh is pricked with a small knife and a meat thermometer registers 165°F. If the skin on the breast of the turkey is overbrowning, cover the turkey with foil, tenting it loosely over the top of the bird to protect the breast.

5. During the last hour of cooking, bake the reserved stuffing, covered with the foil, removing the foil after ½ hour of roasting. Transfer the turkey to a heated platter, cover loosely with foil and let rest for 20 minutes.

6. **Meanwhile, make the gravy:** Skim the fat from the roasting pan, add the flour and cook over medium-low heat, stirring, until golden. Add the stock in a thin stream, whisking. Add the tomato paste, bay leaf, thyme and sage and bring to a boil. Reduce the heat to low and simmer, stirring occasionally, for 20 minutes, or until lightly thickened. Season the gravy with Worcestershire sauce and salt and pepper to taste and strain into a sauceboat.

7. Remove the strings from the turkey, carve and serve with the additional stuffing and gravy on the side.

❖ To toast pecans, place in a small, dry skillet over medium heat and toast, stirring occasionally, for 3 to 5 minutes, or until fragrant. Remove from the skillet and let cool.

Roasted Pearl Onion *and* Raisin Compote

Makes 6 cups, serving 6 to 8
Preparation time: 20 minutes (to peel the onions)
Cooking time: 1 hour 5 minutes

THIS SWEET-AND-SOUR CONDIMENT is very good with poultry, roasted meats and even fish. It keeps well in an airtight container in the refrigerator and, packed decoratively, makes a nice gift during the holidays.

You will need to blanch the pearl onions to make it easier to peel them: Plunge them into a saucepan of boiling water and boil for 1 minute, or until the skins wrinkle. Drain, let cool and slip off the skins. Do not try to peel them without blanching them first.

1½	pounds small white onions, peeled
2	tablespoons olive oil
	Salt and freshly ground black pepper
⅔	cup dry white wine
1½	cups dark raisins
1½	cups canned crushed tomatoes in puree (from a 16-ounce can)
3	garlic cloves, minced
1	tablespoon sugar
1	sprig fresh thyme, or 1 teaspoon dried, crumbled
1	bay leaf
3	tablespoons minced fresh parsley

1. Preheat the oven to 425°F.

2. In a roasting pan, toss the onions with the oil and salt and pepper to taste and roast for 25 to 30 minutes, stirring occasionally, or until golden brown. Transfer the onions to a saucepan.

3. Add the wine to the roasting pan. Bring to a boil and boil for 1 minute to reduce the liquid, then add to the onions. Add the raisins, tomatoes, garlic, sugar, thyme, bay leaf and salt and pepper to taste. If necessary, add water to cover the onions completely. Bring to a boil, reduce the heat to low and simmer over low heat, stirring occasionally, for 30 minutes, or until the onions are tender. Discard the bay leaf.

4. Let cool to room temperature and stir in the parsley. Store, covered, in the refrigerator for up to 1 week.

Chapter V

Meat

MEAT IS THE FOOD MOST COMMONLY ASSOCIATED with roasting, but as with poultry, opinions on how best to do it vary. Does the combination of a higher oven temperature with a shorter cooking time guarantee more tender, juicy results? Or is a lower temperature with a longer cooking time the key to an exquisitely cooked cut? The answer to both questions is yes. It is not a single method of roasting that determines success, but matching the right method to the proper cut.

Generally speaking, the more tender the cut, the higher the temperature and the shorter the cooking time. For example, a two-pound sirloin steak, such as Beef Sirloin Steak with Horseradish Sauce (page 150), can roast to perfection at 500°F in about eight minutes, while a less tender cut of sirloin tip requires a lower temperature and slower roasting time—more than an hour.

Obviously, the larger the cut, the longer the cooking time. We roast a four-pound boneless loin of pork, after an initial browning at 450°F, for one and a half hours at 325°F, while pork tenderloins, each weighing up to one pound, cook best at 425°F for a considerably shorter time. Similarly, a bone-in leg of lamb is browned at high heat and then roasted at a lower temperature, while a butterflied leg of lamb, which has no bone, is roasted at high heat for a shorter time. Both lamb shoulder and breast, which are tougher cuts, require longer cooking at lower temperatures.

Bear in mind that pork, which is now bred to be much lower in fat than in former days, and veal, which is young and tender, have the tendency to dry out very quickly and become tough. Because most people prefer these meats medium rather than rare, a slower oven temperature ensures that they will cook to the proper doneness.

The cornerstone of this chapter is the standing rib roast, the center of Sunday lunch week after week when we were children. We've dressed it up with a shiitake mushroom sauce. Less sophisticated but no less delicious is the roast beef with root vegetables and old-fashioned gravy. Homey and comforting, it is another of our favorites.

Meat

Prime Rib *of* Beef *with* Shiitake Mushroom Sauce

Serves 8

Preparation time: 20 minutes ❖ *Cooking time: 2½ hours*

CERTAIN CUTS OF MEAT are tailor-made for easy roasting, and standing rib roast of beef (prime rib) is one of them. Unless you brazenly overcook it, it is almost impossible to ruin. (We do suggest using a meat thermometer.)

Shiitake mushroom sauce adds to the overall specialness of this roast. You can make the sauce ahead of time, then pour in any rendered juices from the roast right before serving and reheat. Potatoes—your favorite kind—make a natural accompaniment, and we like old-fashioned creamed spinach with this too.

For the beef

1   10-to-10½-pound trimmed standing rib roast, at room temperature

1   teaspoon dried, crumbled thyme

Salt

Crushed black peppercorns

3   medium-to-large onions, quartered

For the shiitake mushroom sauce

2   tablespoons unsalted butter

½   cup minced shallots (3-4 large)

½   pound shiitake mushrooms, trimmed and sliced

Salt and freshly ground black pepper

2   garlic cloves, minced

3   cups homemade or canned beef stock

1   bay leaf

1   sprig fresh thyme or 1 teaspoon dried, crumbled

1   tablespoon tomato paste

½   cup dry white wine

3   tablespoons Sercial Madeira

2   tablespoons arrowroot

Fresh thyme sprigs, for garnish (optional)

1. **Prepare the beef:** Preheat the oven to 500°F.

2. Season the rib roast with the thyme and salt and pepper to taste and place in a large roasting pan. Roast for 30 minutes, then reduce the heat to 350°F and roast for 1¾ to 2 hours more, or until a meat thermometer registers 130°F for medium-rare. After the roast has cooked for about 1½ hours, add the onions to the roasting pan and turn to coat them with the pan juices.

3. **Meanwhile, make the shiitake mushroom sauce:** In a medium saucepan, melt the butter over medium heat. Add the shallots and cook, stirring, for 2 minutes, or until softened. Add the mushrooms and salt and pepper to taste and cook, stirring occasionally, for 7 minutes, or until the mushroom juices have been released and have evaporated. Add the garlic and cook, stirring, for 1 minute more, or until fragrant. Add the stock, bay leaf, thyme and tomato paste and bring to a boil. Reduce the heat to low and simmer, stirring occasionally, for 30 minutes, to blend the flavors. Remove from the heat.

4. When the roast is done, transfer it to a platter with the onions, cover loosely with foil and let stand for 20 minutes. Pour off the fat from the roasting pan. Add the wine and bring to a boil, scraping up the brown bits that cling to the bottom and sides. Strain the liquid into the simmering sauce.

5. In a small bowl, stir the Madeira and arrowroot together. Bring the sauce to a boil and add the Madeira mixture in a thin stream, whisking. Reduce the heat to low and simmer, stirring occasionally, until lightly thickened, 1 to 2 minutes. Discard the bay leaf and the thyme sprig, if used. Pour any juices that have accumulated around the roast into the sauce.

6. Garnish the roast and onions with fresh thyme sprigs, if desired, and nap the onions with some of the sauce. Serve the remaining sauce separately.

Mother's Roast Beef *with* Root Vegetables *and* Old-Fashioned Gravy

Serves 6 to 8

Preparation time: 20 minutes ❖ *Cooking time: 70 minutes*

MEMORIES OF MANY OF THE MEALS we grew up on fade over time, but time cannot erase the really great ones. Here is such a meal. There's nothing fancy about it. It's delicious, reliable, old-fashioned fare: meat and vegetables, which both of our mothers knew how to cook.

Aside from the obvious ease and convenience of a being a meal-in-one, this brings the added pleasure of a variety of vegetables that have roasted in the succulent pan juices. The gravy is a winner too. Sirloin tip is the preferred cut, but eye of round roast is a very acceptable substitute.

For the roast beef

1	3-pound beef sirloin tip or eye of round roast, wrapped in a thin layer of fat and tied (see Tip)
2	garlic cloves, cut into thin slivers, plus 6 whole cloves
	Salt and freshly ground black pepper
4	carrots, cut into 2-inch lengths
4	white turnips, quartered
3	Idaho potatoes, cut into 2-inch pieces
2	onions, cut into eighths
½	teaspoon dried, crumbled thyme
½	teaspoon dried, crumbled marjoram
3	tablespoons olive oil

For the old-fashioned gravy

3	cups homemade or canned beef stock
1	tablespoon tomato paste
¼	teaspoon dried, crumbled thyme
¼	teaspoon dried, crumbled marjoram
2	tablespoons soy sauce
	Worcestershire sauce
3	tablespoons flour
2	tablespoons minced fresh parsley, for garnish

1. **Prepare the roast beef:** Preheat the oven to 450°F.

2. Pat the roast dry with paper towels. Make slits in its surface with a sharp knife and insert a sliver of garlic into each slit. Season the meat with salt and pepper.

3. In a roasting pan, combine the carrots, turnips, potatoes, onions, whole garlic cloves, dried herbs, and salt and pepper to taste. Add the oil and toss to coat the vegetables. Scatter the vegetables around the outside edge of the pan, then place the meat in the middle.

4. Roast for 30 minutes, until the beef and vegetables are browned. Reduce the oven temperature to 350°F and roast, stirring the vegetables occasionally, for 30 minutes more for rare, 40 minutes for medium-rare. Transfer the meat and all the vegetables except the onions and garlic to a serving platter. Cover the roast loosely with foil and let it rest while making the gravy.

5. **Make the gravy:** Pour off the fat from the roasting pan, leaving the onions and garlic in the pan. Add the stock and bring to a boil, scraping up the brown bits on the bottom of the pan, then add the tomato paste, dried herbs, soy sauce and Worcestershire to taste. Bring to a boil, reduce the heat to low and simmer, stirring occasionally and mashing the garlic with the back of a fork, for 10 minutes.

6. Meanwhile, in a small bowl, whisk together the flour and ¼ cup cold water. Add the flour mixture to the gravy in a thin stream, whisking, and simmer for 5 minutes more, or until lightly thickened. Stir any juices that have collected around the roast into the gravy.

7. Remove any fat, if necessary, and the strings from the meat and cut the roast into thin slices. Arrange the slices on a platter with the vegetables and sprinkle the vegetables with the parsley. Serve the gravy in a sauceboat.

❖ Both the sirloin tip and the eye-of-round roast are lean cuts; ask your butcher to wrap them in a thin layer of fat to protect them from the high heat.

Beef Sirloin Steak *with* Horseradish Sauce

Serves 6
Preparation time: 40 minutes (includes draining the yogurt and making the sauce)
Cooking time: 11 minutes

BEEF AND HORSERADISH SAUCE is a combination hard to improve upon. Horseradish goes as well with steak as with a standing rib roast, and, needless to say, steak cooks far more quickly.

For the beef sirloin
1   2-pound boneless lean sirloin steak, cut 2 inches thick
    Salt and freshly ground black pepper
1   tablespoon vegetable oil

For the horseradish sauce
½   cup sour cream
½   cup low-fat plain yogurt, drained (see Tip, page 40)
¼   cup grated peeled fresh horseradish, or bottled horseradish, drained
2   tablespoons white wine vinegar
    Pinch of sugar
    Salt to taste

1. **Prepare the beef sirloin:** Preheat the oven to 500°F.

2. Pat the meat dry, then season it with salt and pepper to taste. Heat a 10-inch cast-iron skillet or other heavy ovenproof skillet over high heat until very hot. Add the oil and heat it until almost smoking. Add the steak and sear it on one side for 1 minute. Turn the steak, place the skillet in the oven and roast for 8 to 10 minutes for rare, or until an instant-read thermometer registers 120°F. Transfer the steak to a serving platter and let it rest for 5 minutes.

3. **Meanwhile, make the horseradish sauce:** In a small serving bowl, combine all the ingredients.

4. Thinly slice the steak and serve it with the sauce on the side.

Roasted Peppered Tenderloin *of* Beef

with Port Wine Sauce

Serves 6 to 8

Preparation time: 10 minutes ❖ *Cooking time: 65 minutes (includes making the sauce)*

FOR MOST OF US, beef tenderloin is the best of all possible cuts, reserved for special occasions—Christmas, New Year's Eve, birthdays and the like. This one is roasted to medium-rare. If you prefer rare, decrease the roasting time to 35 minutes; an instant-read thermometer should register 120°F for rare.

Ruby port is nonvintage, fruity in flavor and affordable. If you have vintage port in your cabinet, by all means use it instead. It will lend even more character to the marvelous pepper sauce

For the tenderloin

- 2 tablespoons coarsely crushed black peppercorns (see Tips)
- 1 teaspoon coarse sea salt or kosher salt
- 1 4-to-4½-pound trimmed beef tenderloin, patted dry and tied (see Tips)
- 2 tablespoons balsamic vinegar

For the sauce

- ½ cup minced shallots (3-4 large)
- 1 cup dry red wine
- 1 teaspoon coarsely crushed black peppercorns
- ½ teaspoon dried, crumbled rosemary
- ½ teaspoon dried, crumbled thyme
- 3 cups homemade or canned beef stock
- 2 tablespoons tomato paste
- 2 tablespoons arrowroot
- 3 tablespoons ruby port

1. **Prepare the beef tenderloin:** Preheat the oven to 500°F.

2. Rub the peppercorns and salt into the tenderloin, sprinkle it with the vinegar and place it in a roasting pan. Roast for 30 to 35 minutes, or until a meat thermometer registers 130°F for medium-rare. Transfer the tenderloin to a serving platter and let stand, loosely tented with foil, for 15 minutes.

3. **Meanwhile, make the sauce:** In a saucepan, combine the shallots, wine, peppercorns and herbs and boil the mixture over high heat to reduce to ½ cup. Add the stock and tomato paste and simmer, stirring occasionally, for 10 minutes to blend the flavors.

4. In a small bowl, stir the arrowroot into the port. Add in a thin stream to the stock mixture, whisking, and simmer until the sauce is lightly thickened, 1 to 2 minutes.

5. Remove the strings from the tenderloin, cut into slices and serve with the sauce in a sauceboat.

❖ Coarse is the operative word here. To crush peppercorns coarsely, put them in a small plastic bag, then press the bottom of a heavy skillet over them. They end up cracked and broken, not ground, which is what you want.

❖ So that the tenderloin will roast evenly, fold the narrow end under the roast and tie the roast with kitchen string at 2-inch intervals.

$\mathcal{R}$oasted Veal Chops *with* Sage

Serves 4
Preparation time: 20 minutes
Cooking time: 30 minutes (includes making the sauce)

EVERYONE RECOGNIZES THE SPECIALNESS OF VEAL—including, alas, its astronomic price. This recipe serves four, putting this dish squarely in the category of elegant company fare. Should you have any trouble finding rib veal chops, substitute loin chops, which are slightly bigger and have a little more meat on them.

This is a dish of subtle flavors, with hints of garlic, tomato and sage. Make the effort to find fresh sage. Sage's affinity with veal is renowned, and while the dried variety will do, it doesn't compare to fresh. The sauce is intentionally light. It serves to nap, not coat. Your favorite polenta dish would be a wonderful foil for the sauce; and for the vegetable, try Roasted Asparagus with Parmesan (page 175).

4	rib veal chops, cut 1 inch thick	⅓	cup minced shallots (2-3 large)
	Flour for dredging	½	cup dry white wine
	Salt and freshly ground black pepper	1	cup homemade or canned beef stock
2	tablespoons olive oil	2	teaspoons tomato paste
4	large garlic cloves, halved	1½	teaspoons arrowroot
4	fresh sage leaves (optional), plus 1 tablespoon minced, or 1 teaspoon dried, crumbled	1	tablespoon Sercial Madeira or dry sherry

1. Preheat the oven to 400°F.

2. Dredge each chop lightly in flour, shake off the excess and season with salt and pepper.

3. In an ovenproof skillet, heat the oil over medium heat until hot. Add the garlic and the whole fresh sage leaves, if using, and cook, stirring, until the garlic is golden and the sage leaves are crisp, about 3 minutes. With a slotted spoon, transfer the garlic and sage to a plate; set aside.

4. Increase the heat to medium-high. Add the veal chops to the skillet and cook for 2 minutes, or until golden brown on the bottom. Turn the chops, sprinkle them with the minced fresh sage or dried, crumbled and return the garlic to the skillet.

5. Transfer the skillet to the oven and roast the chops for 12 minutes, or until springy to the touch. Transfer the chops to a serving platter and keep warm.

6. Add the shallots to the skillet and cook over medium-high heat, stirring, for 2 minutes, or until softened. Add the wine and boil over high heat to reduce by half, about 3 minutes. Stir in the stock and tomato paste, reduce the heat to low and simmer, pressing the garlic into the sauce, for 5 minutes, or until flavorful.

7. In a small bowl, combine the arrowroot with the Madeira or sherry. Add it to the skillet and simmer, stirring, until lightly thickened, 1 to 2 minutes. Strain the sauce over the chops, garnish the platter with the whole crisped sage leaves (if used) and serve.

*L*oin *of* Pork Roasted *with* Honey *and* Mustard

Serves 6

Preparation time: 15 minutes ❖ *Cooking time: 1 hour 50 minutes*

THE SWEETNESS OF PORK is punctuated by the bite of mustard—a simple combination that is nonetheless delicious. If you want, while the finished roast is resting, defat the cooking juices in the roasting pan, add one cup of stock or beef broth to the pan to deglaze it and then strain the gravy into a sauceboat.

A dark green vegetable, such as broccoli or brussels sprouts, would contrast nicely with the paleness of the pork. Mashed potatoes—sweet or white—complete the plate.

2 garlic cloves, minced	Salt and freshly ground black pepper
1 teaspoon minced fresh rosemary, or ½ teaspoon dried, crumbled	1 4-pound boneless center-cut loin of pork, patted dry
1 teaspoon minced fresh sage, or ½ teaspoon dried, crumbled	½ cup honey
1 teaspoon minced fresh thyme, or ½ teaspoon dried, crumbled	3 tablespoons Dijon mustard
	1 tablespoon fresh lemon juice

1. Preheat the oven to 450°F.

2. In a small bowl, combine the garlic, rosemary, sage, thyme and salt and pepper to taste. Rub the mixture all over the pork. Place the pork in a roasting pan and roast for 20 minutes, or until browned.

3. While the meat is browning, combine the honey, mustard and lemon juice in a small bowl.

4. Lower the oven temperature to 325°F, brush the pork with the honey mixture and continue roasting, basting with the pan juices, for 1¼ to 1½ hours more, or until cooked through and a meat thermometer registers 155°F. Remove the pork from the oven and let stand, loosely covered, for 15 minutes before carving.

Brown-Sugar-*and*-Soy-Marinated

Roast Pork Tenderloin

Serves 6
Preparation time: 2¼ hours (includes marinating the pork)
Cooking time: 30 minutes

PORK TENDERLOIN IS PERFECT for roasting on high heat, with two caveats: Be careful not to overcook it—it can dry out—and marinate it before cooking.

In this recipe, a garlicky soy-based marinade adds flavor, so all you need to do is roast and baste occasionally. Leftovers, if you have any, are particularly good in sandwiches. Use crusty bread, spread it with sesame mayonnaise and add a leaf or two of arugula. Serve with Roasted Red Onions and Peppers with Cilantro (page 186).

For the marinade
⅓ cup vegetable oil
¼ cup dry sherry
3 tablespoons reduced-sodium soy sauce
3 tablespoons light or dark brown sugar
1 teaspoon grated lime zest
3 tablespoons fresh lime juice
3 garlic cloves, minced
1 tablespoon minced fresh cilantro

For the tenderloins
2 ¾-to-1-pound pork tenderloins
Salt and freshly ground black pepper

1. **Make the marinade:** In a shallow nonreactive dish, combine all the marinade ingredients. Add the tenderloins and turn to coat them. Cover and marinate in the refrigerator for at least 2 hours, or overnight.

2. **Prepare the tenderloins:** Preheat the oven to 425°F.

3. Remove the tenderloins from the marinade, reserving the marinade, pat dry with paper towels and season with salt and pepper. Place the tenderloins in a roasting pan and roast, basting occasionally with the marinade, for 30 minutes, or until cooked through and an instant-read thermometer registers 155°F. Transfer the tenderloins to a serving platter and let rest for 5 minutes before slicing.

*P*ork Sausages Roasted *with* Onions *and* Apples

Serves 4
Preparation time: 10 minutes ❖ *Cooking time: 40 minutes*

WE LOVE SAUSAGES, but panfrying them gets a little tedious—to say nothing of what it does to the stovetop. Roasting them, on the other hand, makes cooking and cleanup easy.

These sausages are a natural with many egg dishes; remember them when planning your next brunch. Serve with good mustard or a Thai peanut sauce.

1½	pounds sweet Italian sausages, lightly pricked with a fork
2	cups sliced onions
2	McIntosh apples, cored, halved and thickly sliced
3	tablespoons unsalted butter, melted

1	tablespoon minced fresh sage, or 1 teaspoon dried, crumbled
	Salt and freshly ground black pepper
3	tablespoons minced fresh parsley

1. Preheat the oven to 425°F. Lightly oil a roasting pan.

2. Place the sausages in a roasting pan and roast, turning occasionally, for 20 minutes.

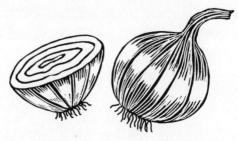

3. Meanwhile, combine the onions and apples with the butter in a large bowl, toss to coat and season with the sage and salt and pepper to taste. Pour off the fat from the roasting pan and add the apple mixture to the pan, scattering it around the sausages. Roast, stirring occasionally, for 20 minutes more, or until the juices run clear when the sausages are pricked with a fork and the onions and apples are golden. Transfer to a large serving plate and sprinkle with the parsley.

Roasted Spareribs Asian Style

Serves 6

Preparation time: 3 hours 20 minutes (includes marinating the ribs) ❖ *Cooking time: 1 hour*

WE'VE RATCHETED UP the flavor of hoisin sauce with garlic and ginger, plus red pepper flakes, and put it to good use as both a marinade and a sauce for ribs. The ribs are roasted at 375°F for the whole cooking time, resulting in meat that virtually falls off the bone. Hold the knives and forks when serving these, but bring on the napkins. Serve this with old-fashioned coleslaw or an Asian-style rice salad.

4	large garlic cloves, minced	3	tablespoons ketchup
1	tablespoon minced fresh ginger	3	tablespoons cider vinegar
⅔	cup reduced-sodium soy sauce	3	tablespoons dry sherry
⅔	cup hoisin sauce	1	teaspoon red pepper flakes, or to taste
¼	cup honey	1	4-pound rack pork spareribs

1. In a shallow, nonreactive baking dish large enough to hold the ribs in a single layer, combine the garlic, ginger, soy sauce, hoisin sauce, honey, ketchup, vinegar, sherry and pepper flakes. Add the ribs, turn to coat, cover and marinate in the refrigerator, turning once, for at least 3 hours, or overnight.

2. Preheat the oven to 375°F.

3. Arrange the ribs on a rack in a roasting pan, reserving the marinade. Roast, basting frequently with the marinade, for 1 hour, or until tender.

4. Transfer the ribs to a cutting board, cut them into several-rib servings with a sharp knife and arrange on a platter.

Roasted Breast *of* Lamb *with* Mustard *and* Herbed Crumbs

Serves 4

Preparation time: 10 minutes ❖ *Cooking time: 40 minutes*

THIS IS GREAT FINGER FOOD, the kind that goes well with potato or macaroni salad or mashed potatoes. Lamb breast, which resembles a rack of pork ribs, is a fatty cut, making these ribs succulent. Blanching the lamb before roasting helps remove excess fat. Mango chutney makes a spirited accompaniment.

1	3-pound breast of lamb	3	tablespoons olive oil
2	garlic cloves, slivered	1½	cups plain dry bread crumbs
	Salt and freshly ground black pepper	2	tablespoons minced fresh rosemary,
2	large eggs, lightly beaten		or 2 teaspoons dried, crumbled
⅓	cup Dijon mustard		

1. Preheat the oven to 500°F. Lightly oil a shallow roasting pan.

2. In a large pot, bring enough water to cover the lamb to a boil. Carefully add the lamb and blanch for 15 minutes. Drain the lamb and pat dry. With the tip of a sharp knife, make incisions all over the lamb. Slip a sliver of garlic into each incision and season with salt and pepper.

3. In a large, shallow bowl, combine the eggs, mustard and 1 tablespoon of the oil. In a separate shallow bowl, combine the bread crumbs and rosemary. Dip the lamb in the egg mixture, then coat it with the herbed crumbs.

4. Place the lamb in the roasting pan and drizzle with the remaining 2 tablespoons oil. Roast for 20 to 25 minutes, or until the crumbs are browned; the meat should be well done. Cut the breast into riblets and transfer to a serving platter.

Glazed Leg *of* Lamb *with* Root Vegetables

Serves 8 to 10
Preparation time: 2 hours 20 minutes (includes marinating the lamb)
Cooking time: 1 hour 45 minutes (includes making the sauce)

IF YOU USUALLY ROAST LEG OF LAMB PLAIN, here is a recipe that is equally simple to put together but includes vegetables too. For maximum flavor, start marinating the lamb the day before you plan to serve it.

1   7½-to-8-pound leg of lamb
4   large garlic cloves, slivered

For the marinade
½   cup Dijon mustard
2   tablespoons olive oil
1   tablespoon minced fresh thyme,
     or 1 teaspoon dried, crumbled
1   tablespoon minced fresh rosemary,
     or 1 teaspoon dried, crumbled
2   tablespoons white wine vinegar
1   tablespoon honey
1   tablespoon soy sauce
1   tablespoon minced fresh ginger

4   large onions, quartered
4   carrots, cut into diagonal slices,
     about ½ inch thick
2   tablespoons olive oil
    Salt and freshly ground black pepper

For the sauce
½   cup dry white wine
2   cups homemade or canned beef stock
1½ tablespoons arrowroot
    Salt and freshly ground black pepper

1. **Prepare the lamb:** Pat the lamb dry with paper towels. With the tip of a sharp knife, make incisions in the meat. Place a sliver of garlic in each incision.

2. **Make the marinade:** In a small bowl, combine the marinade ingredients. Place the lamb in a shallow nonreactive dish and pour the marinade over it, coating the entire surface. Cover and marinate in the refrigerator for at least 2 hours, or overnight, turning once.

3. Preheat the oven to 450°F.

4. Transfer the lamb to a shallow roasting pan and brush it with some of the marinade; discard the remaining marinade. In a bowl, toss the onions and carrots with the oil and salt and pepper to taste. Arrange the vegetables around the lamb and roast for 20 minutes, or until they are browned. Reduce the oven temperature to 350°F and roast for 1¼ hours more, basting with the pan juices, or until a meat thermometer registers 130°F for medium-rare.

5. Transfer the lamb to a platter and let stand, loosely covered, for 15 minutes. Transfer the vegetables to a heatproof dish and keep warm in the oven set at the lowest temperature.

6. **Make the sauce:** Remove the fat from the pan with a large spoon, or use a gravy separator, if desired. Add the wine to the juices in the roasting pan and bring to a boil, scraping up the brown bits on the bottom. Add the stock, bring to a boil, reduce the heat to low and simmer for 5 minutes to blend the flavors.

7. In a small bowl, combine the arrowroot with 3 tablespoons water. Add the arrowroot in a thin stream to the stock mixture, whisking. Simmer, whisking, until lightly thickened, 1 to 2 minutes. Season with salt and pepper to taste. Strain the sauce into a sauceboat.

8. Pour any juices that have collected around the lamb into the sauce. Surround the lamb with the roasted vegetables. Serve with the sauce.

Roasted Butterflied Leg *of* Lamb

with English Mint Sauce

Serves 8 to 10

Preparation time: 2¼ hours (includes marinating the lamb)

Cooking time: 25 minutes

FEW CUTS OF MEAT ARE AS FESTIVE AS butterflied leg of lamb—or more suitable for company. This recipe recommends itself for entertaining; the cooking time is all of 25 minutes.

The mint sauce will be something of a conversation piece. It is saucy, nothing like mint jelly, and, in our opinion, a decided improvement on it. Roasted Sugar Snap Peas (page 194) are good with this, as are scalloped potatoes. The peas can roast while the lamb rests.

For the lamb

- 1 7-pound leg of lamb, boned and butterflied
- 4 garlic cloves, minced
- 1 tablespoon minced fresh rosemary, or 2 teaspoons dried, crumbled
- 1 tablespoon minced fresh thyme, or 2 teaspoons dried, crumbled
- 3 tablespoons olive oil

For the mint sauce

- 3½ cups loosely packed fresh mint leaves, chopped
- 3½ tablespoons sugar, or more to taste
- ⅔ cup malt vinegar or cider vinegar
  Salt and freshly ground black pepper

1. **Prepare the lamb:** Pat the lamb dry with paper towels and place it in a large baking dish. In a small bowl, combine the garlic, rosemary, thyme and oil. Rub the mixture over both sides of the lamb. Cover and marinate in the refrigerator for at least 2 hours, or overnight.

2. **Make the mint sauce:** In a medium bowl, combine the mint and sugar with ⅔ cup boiling water; stir until the sugar is dissolved. Add the vinegar and let stand at room temperature for 1 hour before serving. (The sauce will keep, covered and chilled, for up to 1 week.)

3. Preheat the oven to 500°F.

4. Season the lamb with salt and pepper. Place the lamb on a rack in a roasting pan and roast, turning once, for 25 minutes for rare, or until a meat thermometer registers 125°F. For medium-rare, the thermometer should register 130°F; for medium, it should register 140°F. Transfer the lamb to a serving platter and cover loosely with foil. Let stand for 10 minutes.

5. Cut the lamb into thin slices and serve with the mint sauce.

*I*ndian-Style Roasted Shoulder *of* Lamb

Serves 6 to 8
Preparation time: 2 hours 20 minutes (includes marinating the lamb)
Cooking time: 45 minutes

DEPENDING UPON HOW WELL STOCKED the meat department of your supermarket is, you may have to special-order a shoulder of lamb. When boned, a 4-pound shoulder should weigh about 2¼ pounds.

Yogurt is frequently used as a marinade for lamb for two reasons: It ameliorates lamb's gaminess and it acts as a tenderizer—important for the shoulder, a cut that is usually tougher than leg meat.

The aromas of the Spice Route—cinnamon, cardamom and cloves—perfume this dish. Serve with rice pilaf. If you have leftover lamb, combine it with minted cucumber rounds in vinegar and serve in pita pockets with a little chutney on the side.

1	4-pound shoulder of lamb, boned (about 2¼ pounds when boned)	1	tablespoon cumin seeds, toasted and ground (see Tip, page 34), or 1½ tablespoons ground cumin
1	tablespoon minced fresh ginger	1	tablespoon ground coriander
6	large garlic cloves, minced	1	teaspoon ground cinnamon
2	cups low-fat plain yogurt	½	teaspoon ground cloves
2	teaspoons salt	½	teaspoon ground cardamom
¼	cup fresh lemon juice	½	teaspoon cayenne pepper

1. Pat the lamb dry with paper towels and place it, boned side up, in a shallow nonreactive baking dish.

2. In a bowl, whisk together the remaining ingredients. Pour the marinade over the lamb and turn to coat it on all sides. Cover and marinate in the refrigerator for at least 2 hours, or overnight, turning once.

3. Preheat the oven to 350°F.

4. Remove the lamb from the marinade, discarding the marinade. Roll the lamb into a cylinder and tie it in several places with kitchen twine. Place the lamb in a roasting pan and roast for 45 minutes, or until a meat thermometer registers 130°F for medium-rare.

5. Transfer the lamb to a cutting board and let rest for 10 minutes. Remove the string from the lamb and cut into slices. Place the slices on a heated platter and serve.

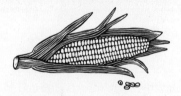

Chapter VI

Vegetables

ROASTING VEGETABLES MAKES them as flavorful as grilling, but with half the hassle—no repeated checking of the weather report to learn whether or not it's going to rain on your barbecue, no preheating of any coals or a gas grill. Many vegetables, like beets or turnips, can be roasted whole without fear of undercooking, while smaller ones can be roasted to tenderness without the bother of losing any pieces between the grates. Choosing to roast vegetables is a way of keeping things simple, an appealing option for busy times.

Boiling vegetables, on the other hand, may be convenient, but it cannot compare with the singular flavor produced by roasting. The dry heat of the oven causes the sugar in root vegetables like carrots and onions to caramelize, intensifying their sweetness. See Roasted Carrots with Ginger (page 178) for a simple, delicious example.

Vegetables that are roasted often need nothing more: no sauce, no topping—except, perhaps, for a drizzle of good olive oil or a sprinkling of fresh herbs. Roasted

Fennel (page 183), for instance, requires only five ingredients, two of them being salt and pepper. Equally easy are Roasted Scallions (page 190), which take just 10 minutes to cook.

Other recipes require slightly more effort. Roasted Winter Squash with Cheddar Cheese (page 198) combines roasted, pureed squash with sharp cheddar in a casserole of complementary opposites. In Bourbon-Glazed Sweet Potato, Apple and Pecan Gratin (page 192), the sweet potatoes are baked, combined with apples, glazed with a spiced mixture of butter, brown sugar and bourbon and roasted. So good is the combination that we feel confident that adding it to your Thanksgiving table will start a lasting tradition.

Vegetables

Roasted Asparagus *with* Parmesan

Serves 4

Preparation time: 15 minutes ❖ *Cooking time: 10 minutes*

ROASTED ASPARAGUS has a marvelous, almost nutlike flavor, quite different from the boiled or steamed. If you have only thin stalks, do not peel them and be careful not to overcook.

1	pound medium-thick asparagus, trimmed and peeled		Salt and freshly ground black pepper
1	tablespoon olive oil	3	tablespoons freshly grated Parmesan

1. Preheat the oven to 500°F.

2. In a shallow roasting pan, toss the asparagus with the oil and salt and pepper to taste, then arrange the spears in a single layer. Roast, turning frequently, for 10 minutes, or until tender and lightly golden.

3. With tongs, transfer the spears to a serving platter. Sprinkle with the Parmesan and serve at once.

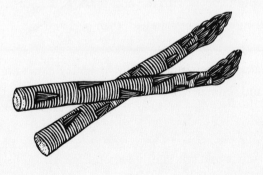

*S*weet-*and*-Sour Roasted Beets

Serves 4 to 6

Preparation time: 15 minutes ❖ *Cooking time: 1¼ hours*

A FRESH BEET TASTES MUCH BETTER than its canned counterpart and a roasted fresh one is better still. To vary the flavor of the sweet-and-sour sauce, experiment with flavored vinegars, such as clove, shallot, rosemary or raspberry.

These beets go well with pot-roasted meat and a big bowl of mashed potatoes.

2	pounds beets (about 6 medium), with 1 inch tops left on, washed		Pinch of ground cloves
2	tablespoons olive oil	2	teaspoons cornstarch
½	cup cider vinegar	2	tablespoons Dijon mustard
⅓	cup honey		Salt and freshly ground black pepper
		1	tablespoon snipped fresh dill

1. Preheat the oven to 400°F.

2. In a shallow baking dish, toss the beets with the oil. Roast for 1 hour, or until tender when pierced with a fork. Let the beets cool enough to be handled, then peel and slice.

3. In a medium, nonreactive saucepan, combine the vinegar, honey, cloves and cornstarch. Bring to a boil over medium heat, whisking, and simmer, whisking, until slightly thickened. Whisk in the mustard and salt and pepper to taste.

4. Add the beet slices to the sauce and stir gently to combine. Bring back to a simmer to heat the beets through. Transfer to a serving dish and sprinkle with the fresh dill.

Roasted Broccoli *with* Lemon Garlic Butter *and* Toasted Pine Nuts

Serves 4

Preparation time: 15 minutes (includes toasting the nuts) ❖ *Cooking time: 12 minutes*

ROASTED BROCCOLI IS FULLER IN FLAVOR than its water-cooked counterpart, and it has a different texture as well.

1	pound broccoli florets (from one 1¼-pound bunch)	2	tablespoons unsalted butter
2	tablespoons olive oil	1	teaspoon minced garlic
	Salt and freshly ground black pepper	½	teaspoon grated lemon zest
		1-2	tablespoons fresh lemon juice
		2	tablespoons pine nuts, toasted (see Tip, page 42)

1. Preheat the oven to 500°F.

2. In a large bowl, toss the broccoli with the oil and salt and pepper to taste. Arrange the florets in a single layer on a baking sheet and roast, turning once, for 12 minutes, or until just tender.

3. Meanwhile, in a small saucepan, melt the butter over medium heat. Add the garlic and the lemon zest and heat, stirring, for about 1 minute. Let cool slightly and stir in the lemon juice.

4. Place the broccoli in a serving bowl, pour the lemon butter over it and toss to coat. Scatter the toasted pine nuts over the top.

Roasted Carrots *with* Ginger

Serves 4

Preparation time: 15 minutes ❖ *Cooking time: 25 minutes*

THIS COMBINATION, SIMPLE AS IT IS, contributes a lot of color and flavor to the Thanksgiving table. If you don't care for cilantro, try fresh mint instead.

1	pound carrots, peeled and halved lengthwise	1	teaspoon grated orange zest
3	tablespoons unsalted butter, melted	1	cup orange juice
1	tablespoon finely grated fresh ginger	1	tablespoon honey
	Salt and freshly ground black pepper	2	tablespoons minced fresh cilantro

1. Preheat the oven to 450°F.

2. In a shallow roasting pan, toss the carrots with 2 tablespoons of the butter, 2 teaspoons of the ginger and salt and pepper to taste. Roast, turning twice, for 15 to 20 minutes, or until tender. Transfer to a serving dish.

3. Add the remaining 1 tablespoon butter and 1 teaspoon ginger, the orange zest and juice and honey to the roasting pan. Simmer over low heat until reduced and lightly thickened, about 5 minutes. Pour the sauce over the carrots, sprinkle with the cilantro and serve.

Corn *on the* Cob Roasted

with Jalapeño-*and*-Cilantro Butter

Serves 8

Preparation time: 20 minutes ❖ *Cooking time: 30 minutes*

WHOLE EARS OF CORN BRUSHED with a butter flavored with chilies and cilantro and roasted in a hot oven in their husks make for incomparable results without the fuss of grilling. One warning: Roasted corn must be eaten as soon as it is cooked, or it will become starchy.

½ cup (1 stick) unsalted butter, softened

2 teaspoons minced fresh or pickled jalapeño chilies

2 tablespoons finely minced fresh cilantro
   Fresh lemon juice

Salt and freshly ground black pepper

8 ears corn

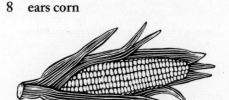

1. Preheat the oven to 500°F.

2. In a bowl, using a fork, mash the butter, chilies, cilantro and lemon juice and salt and pepper to taste into a paste. (The seasoned butter can be prepared up to 3 hours in advance.)

3. Peel the husk back from each ear of corn and remove and discard the silk, but leave each ear in its husk. Spread each ear with some of the flavored butter, then wrap the ears back up in the husks. Arrange the ears in a single layer on a baking sheet and roast, turning occasionally, for 20 to 30 minutes, or until tender. Serve at once.

Roasted Cauliflower

with Capers *and* Brown Butter

Serves 6
Preparation time: 15 minutes (includes roasting the pepper)
Cooking time: 30 minutes

BROWNED BUTTER LENDS AN AIR OF ELEGANCE to anything it adorns, and this combination of cauliflower, bell pepper, olives and capers is no exception. Serve as an accompaniment to roasted meat or fish, such as Loin of Pork Roasted with Honey and Mustard (page 156) or Roasted Halibut Steaks with Herbed Potato Crust (page 96).

1 head cauliflower (about 2 pounds), cut into florets	2 tablespoons drained capers
4 tablespoons (½ stick) unsalted butter	2 tablespoons minced fresh parsley
½ cup minced shallots or scallions	2 tablespoons finely chopped kalamata or other Greek olives
1 tablespoon minced garlic	Salt and freshly ground black pepper
1 red bell pepper, roasted (see page 39), peeled, cored, seeded and diced	2-3 tablespoons plain dry bread crumbs

1. Preheat the oven to 425°F. Butter a 9-x-13-inch baking dish.

2. Bring a medium pot of salted water to a boil. Add the cauliflower florets and blanch for 5 minutes. Drain.

3. In a large skillet, cook the butter over medium heat until golden brown. Add the shallots or scallions and garlic and cook, stirring occasionally, for 2 minutes, or until softened. Add the bell pepper, capers, parsley and olives and cook, stirring, for 1 minute. Add the cauliflower and season with salt and pepper.

4. Transfer to the baking dish, sprinkle with the bread crumbs and roast for 15 to 20 minutes, or until the crumbs are golden.

$\mathcal{R}$oasted Eggplant *and* Tomato Sauce

Makes about 3 cups

Preparation time: 5 minutes ❖ *Cooking time: 48 minutes*

WE LIKE SPAGHETTI BEST with this sauce, which makes enough for one pound of pasta. That should serve two to three hungry people or four to six with smaller appetites. Make a double batch, and freeze what you don't use. You can also use this sauce to dress up a plain omelette.

1 large eggplant (1½ pounds), trimmed and halved lengthwise	1 28-ounce can crushed tomatoes in puree
⅓ cup olive oil	Salt and freshly ground black pepper
1 medium-to-large onion, minced	2 tablespoons minced fresh basil
1 tablespoon minced garlic	

1. Preheat the oven to 400°F. Lightly oil a baking sheet.

2. Place the eggplant on the baking sheet, cut side down, and roast for 20 to 25 minutes, or until the flesh is just tender when tested with a fork. Cool, scoop out the flesh and coarsely chop; discard the peel.

3. In a large skillet, heat the oil over medium heat until hot. Add the onion and garlic and cook, stirring, for 3 minutes, or until softened. Add the tomatoes and simmer, stirring occasionally, for 5 minutes, or until thickened. Add the eggplant and salt and pepper to taste and simmer, stirring occasionally, for 10 to 15 minutes, or until tender. Stir in the basil and serve.

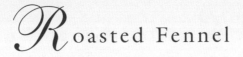oasted Fennel

Serves 6 to 8

Preparation time: 5 minutes ❖ *Cooking time: 40 minutes*

MORE AND MORE PEOPLE are discovering the licoricelike taste of fennel, but it is still something of an unsung treasure. In supermarkets, it is frequently, though incorrectly, called anise. Look for the feathery fronded bulbs, then make this dish to serve with roasted fish or poultry. Snip the fronds and use them in salad.

4   fennel bulbs, rinsed and quartered

2   tablespoons olive oil
    Salt and freshly ground black pepper

2   tablespoons minced fresh parsley
    or fennel fronds

1. Preheat the oven to 450°F. Lightly oil a shallow roasting pan.

2. Brush the fennel with the oil and season with salt and pepper to taste. Arrange in the pan and roast, turning twice, for 35 to 40 minutes, or until golden brown and tender. Sprinkle with the parsley and serve.

Roasted Green Beans

Serves 4

Preparation time: 10 minutes ❖ *Cooking time: 15 minutes*

ROASTING PUTS A NEW SPIN ON GREEN BEANS. Select beans that are a uniform medium size. Avoid big, lanky ones; they don't roast well. It is important to arrange the beans in a single layer in the pan; otherwise, they will cook unevenly.

1½	pounds green beans, trimmed	Salt and freshly ground black pepper
2	tablespoons olive oil	

1. Preheat the oven to 500°F.

2. In a bowl, toss the beans with the oil and salt and pepper to taste. Arrange the beans in a single layer on a baking sheet and roast, turning occasionally, for 12 to 15 minutes, or until just tender. Serve at once.

Slow-Roasted Onions

Makes 4 cups, serving 4 to 6
Preparation time: 5 minutes ❖ *Cooking time: 1 hour*

THESE ONIONS ARE SUPERB with any kind of roasted meat, with soft scrambled eggs or as a topping for toasted French bread. The long, slow cooking brings out the sweetness of the onions. Vidalia onions are especially good in this recipe.

6	large onions, each about 4 inches in diameter (do not peel)	2	tablespoons balsamic vinegar
2	tablespoons olive oil	3	tablespoons minced fresh parsley
2-3	tablespoons unsalted butter, softened		Salt and freshly ground black pepper

1. Preheat the oven to 350°F.

2. With the tip of a sharp knife, prick each onion all over. In a shallow roasting dish, toss the onions with just enough olive oil to coat them. Roast for 1 hour, or until tender.

3. Halve the onions, remove the skins and roots and cut into slices. Place the slices in a serving dish and toss with the butter, vinegar, parsley, salt to taste and lots of pepper. Serve immediately.

Roasted Red Onions *and* Peppers *with* Cilantro

Serves 6

Preparation time: 10 minutes ❖ *Cooking time: 30 minutes*

IT'S NO SECRET THAT PEPPERS AND ONIONS go well together. This recipe is loosely modeled upon a popular Italian stovetop dish but contains far less oil. If you have any leftovers, slice them and serve on rounds of toasted whole-grain bread or hot pasta.

3	large red bell peppers, cored, seeded and quartered	3	tablespoons olive oil
			Salt and freshly ground black pepper
3	large green bell peppers, cored, seeded and quartered	2	garlic cloves, sliced
2	large red onions, quartered	1-2	tablespoons fresh lemon juice
		2	tablespoons minced fresh cilantro

1. Preheat the oven to 425°F.

2. In a large roasting pan, combine the peppers and onions with the oil and salt and pepper to taste; toss to coat. Roast, tossing occasionally, for 25 to 30 minutes, or until the vegetables are tender. During the last 10 minutes of cooking time, add the garlic and roast until softened.

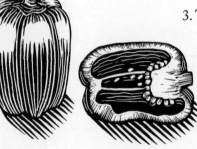

3. Transfer the vegetables to a serving dish, sprinkle with the lemon juice and cilantro and toss to combine.

$\mathcal{R}$oasted Parsnip Ribbons

Serves 4 to 6

Preparation time: 10 minutes ❖ *Cooking time: 18 minutes*

PARSNIPS LOOK LIKE BIG OFF-WHITE CARROTS but are sweeter in flavor. Depending upon how thick you cut them, these sweet roasted parsnip strips can be crunchy or tender. They're good with almost any roasted meat or poultry.

1	pound parsnips	Salt and freshly ground black pepper
2	tablespoons vegetable oil	

1. Preheat the oven to 450°F.

2. Peel the parsnips with a vegetable peeler. With the peeler, cut the parsnips lengthwise into strips about ⅛ inch thick. In a bowl, combine the strips with the oil and salt and pepper to taste and toss.

3. Arrange the strips in a single layer on a baking sheet. Roast for 10 minutes; turn with tongs and roast for 8 minutes more, or until crisp. Sprinkle with more salt, if desired, before serving.

Roasted Potatoes *with* Onions, Green Pepper *and* Pimento

Serves 4

Preparation time: 15 minutes ❖ *Cooking time: 33 minutes*

OVEN-ROASTED POTATOES are almost impossible to resist, and this casserole, with onion, bell pepper and pimento, is hard to stop eating. It's colorful and healthful, especially compared with hash browns sautéed in oil.

1   pound Idaho potatoes (about 2 large), scrubbed and cut into ½-inch dice

1   large onion, diced

1   green bell pepper, cored, seeded and cut into ½-inch dice

1   tablespoon olive oil

2   tablespoons unsalted butter, softened
    Salt and freshly ground black pepper

1   4-ounce jar pimentos, drained and diced

2   tablespoons minced fresh parsley

1. Preheat the oven to 425°F. Lightly oil a large baking dish.

2. In a bowl, toss together the potatoes, onion, bell pepper, oil, butter and salt and pepper to taste. Spread the vegetables in the baking dish in a single layer and roast, stirring occasionally, for 25 minutes.

3. Add the pimentos and roast for 8 minutes more, or until the potatoes are golden. Sprinkle with the parsley and serve.

Roasted Potato Cakes

Makes 8 cakes, serving 4
Preparation time: 20 minutes (includes making the Cilantro Cream)
Cooking time: 35 minutes

WE LOVE POTATO PANCAKES and serve them for breakfast, lunch and dinner, or for snacks in between. Because these pancakes are roasted rather than fried, they are less greasy than traditional versions, with a more pronounced potato flavor. The cilantro cream is optional, but it is especially good when you are serving these as a first course—in which case, you should form smaller patties.

2 pounds Idaho potatoes (4 large), peeled, grated and squeezed dry

½ cup minced scallions

2 tablespoons flour

1 tablespoon minced fresh rosemary, or 1 teaspoon dried, crumbled

Salt

Cayenne pepper

4 tablespoons (½ stick) unsalted butter, melted, for brushing the cakes

Cilantro Cream (page 64), for serving (optional)

1. Preheat the oven to 450°F. Lightly oil 2 baking sheets.

2. In a large bowl, combine the potatoes, scallions, flour, rosemary and salt and cayenne to taste. Form the mixture into cakes 4 to 5 inches in diameter and ⅓ inch thick, and place 3 inches apart on the baking sheets.

3. Brush the tops of the cakes with butter and roast for 20 minutes, or until golden brown on the bottom. Turn, brush the other sides with butter and roast for 10 to 15 minutes more, or until golden brown and crisp. Transfer to a platter and serve hot, with the cilantro cream, if desired.

Roasted Scallions

Serves 4

Preparation time: 5 minutes ❖ *Cooking time: 10 minutes*

SERVE THESE SCALLIONS with a dipping sauce or as part of an antipasto platter with fennel and mushrooms dressed with vinaigrette.

16	scallions (about 3 bunches), trimmed	Salt and freshly ground black pepper
1	tablespoon olive oil	

1. Preheat the oven to 500°F.

2. Brush the scallions with the oil, season with salt and pepper and arrange in a single layer on a baking sheet. Roast for 10 minutes, or until just tender. Serve at once.

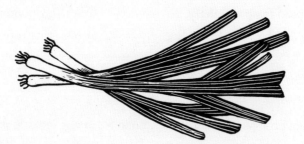

Roasted Sweet Potatoes *and* Garlic *with* Rosemary

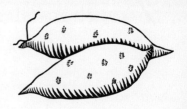

Serves 4

Preparation time: 15 minutes ❖ *Cooking time: 35 minutes*

IF YOU ARE ACCUSTOMED TO MASHED SWEET POTATOES, wait until you taste roasted ones. The outsides turn crisp, the insides appealingly soft. They are slightly crunchy and very sweet.

This dish make a fine accompaniment to the Thanksgiving turkey and can be cooked while the bird is standing waiting to be carved.

1½ pounds sweet potatoes (4 medium), peeled and cut into ½-inch-thick slices	1 tablespoon unsalted butter
6 garlic cloves (do not peel)	2 teaspoons minced fresh rosemary, or 1 teaspoon dried, crumbled
2 tablespoons olive oil	Salt and freshly ground black pepper

1. Preheat the oven to 425°F.

2. Arrange the sweet potatoes and garlic in a shallow flameproof baking dish large enough to hold them in a single layer. Add just enough water to cover the vegetables. Bring the water to a boil over medium-high heat and simmer for 2 minutes. Drain in a colander.

3. In the baking dish, combine the oil and butter and melt the butter over medium heat. Remove from the heat, add the potatoes and garlic, the rosemary and salt and pepper to taste and toss to coat. Spread the potatoes in a single layer and roast on the lowest rack of the oven, turning them occasionally, for 25 to 30 minutes, or until golden brown. Transfer to a heated serving bowl and serve at once.

*B*ourbon-Glazed Sweet Potato, Apple *and* Pecan Gratin

Serves 6
Preparation time: 15 minutes ❖ *Cooking time: 1¼ hours*

S ERVE THIS GRATIN with the Thanksgiving turkey. It has a harvest feel and couldn't be easier to prepare. The edges of the sweet potato and apple slices glow from the delectable glaze.

2 pounds sweet potatoes (about 4), pricked	4 tablespoons (½ stick) unsalted butter
2 Golden Delicious apples, peeled, cored and sliced	⅓ cup firmly packed light brown sugar
	⅓ cup honey
3 tablespoons fresh lemon juice	2 tablespoons bourbon
1 cup pecan halves	1 teaspoon ground cinnamon
	¼ teaspoon ground ginger

1. Preheat the oven to 400°F. Butter a 9-x-12-inch gratin dish.

2. Bake the sweet potatoes on the oven rack for 45 minutes, or until tender. Let cool, then peel and cut into ¼-inch-thick slices on the diagonal. (Leave the oven on.)

3. In a bowl, toss the apples with the lemon juice. Arrange the sweet potatoes and apples, overlapping the slices, in the gratin dish and sprinkle with the pecans.

4. In a small saucepan, combine the remaining ingredients and simmer over medium heat, stirring, until the sugar is dissolved, 2 to 3 minutes. Spoon the glaze over the sweet potatoes and apples.

5. Roast, basting occasionally with the cooking juices, for 30 minutes, or until the apples are tender.

6. Preheat the broiler. Place the dish under the broiler, about 4 inches from the heat, and broil until golden brown; watch carefully. Serve from the gratin dish.

$\mathcal{R}$oasted Sugar Snap Peas

Serves 4 to 6
Preparation time: 10 minutes ❖ *Cooking time: 4 minutes*

W E LOVE SUGAR SNAP PEAS, and they are particularly good roasted.

1	pound sugar snap peas, trimmed and stringed	1	tablespoon unsalted butter, softened
1	tablespoon vegetable oil	2	tablespoons snipped fresh chives or scallion tops, for garnish
	Salt and freshly ground black pepper		

1. Preheat the oven to 450°F.

2. In a shallow roasting pan, toss the peas with the oil and salt and pepper to taste. Roast, stirring once, for 3 to 4 minutes, or until just tender. Transfer to a serving bowl, toss with the butter and garnish with the chives or scallions.

Roasted Italian Tomatoes

Serves 6

Preparation time: 20 minutes ❖ *Cooking time: 1½ hours*

YOU WILL NEED MORE THAN AN HOUR for this "slow-roast." When cooked, the tomatoes will look wrinkled and shriveled. Don't be put off. They have absolutely delicious flavor because of the concentration of their juices over the long cooking time. Serve them with broiled or roasted fish, meat or poultry. They are also very good for brunch, as an accompaniment to a frittata or omelette.

6 large Italian plum tomatoes
     (1½-2 pounds), halved
     lengthwise and seeded
3 small garlic cloves, minced
1 tablespoon minced fresh thyme,
     or 1 teaspoon dried, crumbled

3 tablespoons olive oil
    Salt and freshly ground black pepper
    Minced fresh basil or parsley,
      for garnish

1. Preheat the oven to 325°F. Lightly oil a gratin dish large enough to hold the tomatoes in a single layer.

2. Arrange the tomatoes, cut side up, in the dish and sprinkle with the garlic, thyme, oil and salt and pepper to taste. Roast them on the middle rack of the oven, basting occasionally with their juices, for 1½ hours, or until browned on the bottom. Sprinkle with the basil or parsley and serve warm.

Roasted Tomatoes Provençale

Serves 4

Preparation time: 20 minutes ❖ *Cooking time: 30 minutes*

THESE TOMATOES MAY BE SIMPLE, but they speak of Provence. Vary the herbs, but try to use fresh ones and be generous with the garlic.

4 medium-to-large ripe tomatoes, cored and halved	Salt and freshly ground black pepper
2 large garlic cloves, finely minced	2-3 tablespoons olive oil
2 teaspoons minced fresh thyme, or 1 teaspoon dried, crumbled	¼ cup minced fresh parsley
	¼ cup plain dry bread crumbs

1. Preheat the oven to 400°F. Lightly oil a gratin dish large enough to hold the tomatoes without crowding.

2. Squeeze the tomato halves gently to remove as much juice as possible, without crushing the flesh. Place the tomatoes in the gratin dish, cut side up, and sprinkle with the garlic, thyme and salt and pepper to taste. Drizzle them with the oil.

3. Roast for 20 minutes. Sprinkle on the parsley and bread crumbs and roast for 10 minutes more, or until the tops are golden. Serve at once.

Roasted Turnips

Serves 4

Preparation time: 5 minutes ❖ *Cooking time: 15 minutes*

MASHED OR PUREED, turnips can't compete with potatoes. Roasting, though, brings out their noticeably sweet flavor and elevates them to a class by themselves. This dish requires very little effort on the part of the cook.

6 turnips (about 2½ pounds), trimmed, peeled and quartered	3 tablespoons olive oil Salt and freshly ground black pepper

1. Preheat the oven to 450°F.

2. In a large bowl, toss the turnips with the oil. Arrange the turnips in a baking pan and season with salt and pepper to taste. Roast, stirring once or twice, for 15 minutes, or until golden brown and tender when tested with a fork. Transfer to a bowl and serve hot.

*R*oasted Winter Squash *with* Cheddar Cheese

Serves 4 to 6

Preparation time: 10 minutes ❖ *Cooking time: 1 hour 5 minutes*

THIS COMFORTING CASSEROLE IS A GOOD MATCH for roasted meats or poultry, perfect for the cooler months of the year.

1 large butternut squash (about 2 pounds), halved lengthwise, seeds and strings removed	3 tablespoons unsalted butter, melted Freshly grated nutmeg Salt and freshly ground black pepper
1 cup loosely packed grated sharp cheddar cheese	3 tablespoons plain dry bread crumbs 3 tablespoons freshly grated Parmesan

1. Preheat the oven to 400°F. Lightly oil a roasting pan and butter a large gratin dish.

2. Cut each squash half lengthwise in half again and place, cut side down, in the roasting pan. Roast for 45 minutes, or until tender when tested with a fork. Let cool, then scrape the flesh into a large bowl. (Leave the oven on.)

3. Add the cheddar, 2 tablespoons of the butter, the nutmeg and salt and pepper to taste to the squash; combine well. Spread the squash mixture in the gratin dish, sprinkle with the bread crumbs and Parmesan and drizzle with the remaining 1 tablespoon butter. Roast for 20 minutes, or until heated through. Serve from the gratin dish.

Roasted Zucchini *with* Red Onion

Serves 4

Preparation time: 15 minutes ❖ *Cooking time: 15 minutes*

SAUTÉED ZUCCHINI SLICES are tasty, but the texture of roasted zucchini—a little crisp on the outside, nice and soft within—sets this dish apart, especially with the caramelized red onions.

4 zucchini (about 2 pounds), halved crosswise and quartered lengthwise	Salt and freshly ground black pepper
1 medium red onion, sliced	2 tablespoons minced fresh basil or parsley
2 tablespoons olive oil	Fresh lemon juice

1. Preheat the oven to 450°F.

2. In a shallow roasting pan, toss the zucchini and onion with the oil and salt and pepper to taste. Roast, stirring occasionally, for 10 to 15 minutes, or until the zucchini is tender. Transfer to a serving bowl and sprinkle with the basil or parsley and lemon juice to taste.

Chapter VII

Salads

*A*SALAD WITH A ROASTED INGREDIENT provides the delight of the unexpected. Roasting potatoes for salad instead of boiling them produces a firm, toothsome texture and a mellow, more complex flavor. Similarly, although we are not particularly enthusiastic about the classic dish of boiled beets on a bed of greens, roasted beets, with a little endive and feta added, are another matter entirely: an exciting and pretty prospect for dinner.

Because salads made with roasted ingredients are fuller-flavored than ordinary ones, they can easily play a starring role. Some make superb first courses, like Roasted Portobello Mushroom and Arugula Salad (page 206), in which deglazed juices from the roasting pan are added to the dressing to give it still more dimension. Roasted Tricolor Pepper Salad with Balsamic Vinegar, Basil and Pine Nuts (page 212) makes a glorious antipasto.

Other salads in this chapter come into their own as main courses. Roasted Stuffed

Chicken Breast Salad (page 218), dressed with Roasted Tomato and Onion Dressing (page 205), and Peppered Tuna Salad Niçoise (page 220)—an elegant variation on the famous Provençal creation—fall into this category. Remember that overcooking will give tasteless and dry results, particularly in the case of the tuna.

The wisdom of the phrase "the better the produce, the better the salad" is never truer than when the main ingredient is first roasted. Firm, fresh portobello mushrooms will impart significantly more taste and aroma, not to mention texture, than will those that have stayed too long on a market shelf. Capitalizing on the increased flavor achieved by roasting, we have tried to keep the amount of fat in the following salads to a minimum. How much oil you use is up to you.

Salads

Roasted Beet, Endive *and* Feta Salad

Serves 4

Preparation time: 10 minutes ❖ *Cooking time: 1 hour*

THIS SALAD, which we like to serve as a starter to a light meal, can also be presented as a main course, with fresh bread and a selection of berries for dessert. Instead of feta, aged goat cheese is also very good, as is ripe Gorgonzola. Try substituting fresh basil or Italian parsley for the dill.

4 medium beets (1¼-1½ pounds), 1 inch of tops left on, washed	½ pound feta cheese, crumbled (about 1½ cups)
2 heads Belgian endive, cut lengthwise into thin slivers	2 tablespoons white wine vinegar
1 bunch watercress, stems trimmed, well washed and patted dry	1 tablespoon Dijon mustard
⅓ cup minced scallions	Salt and freshly ground black pepper
	⅓ cup extra-virgin olive oil, or to taste
	2 tablespoons snipped fresh dill

1. Preheat the oven to 400°F.

2. Place the beets in a shallow baking pan and roast for 1 hour, or until tender. Let cool enough to handle, then peel and slice.

3. Divide the endive and watercress among 4 individual salad plates. Top with the sliced beets and sprinkle with the scallions and feta.

4. In a small bowl, whisk together the vinegar, mustard and salt and pepper to taste. Add the oil in a stream, whisking, and whisk the dressing until combined well. Drizzle the dressing over the salads, sprinkle with the dill and serve.

Roasted Tomato *and* Onion Dressing

Makes 3½ cups

Preparation time: 5 minutes ❖ *Cooking time: 15 minutes*

USE THIS MARVELOUS DRESSING for any kind of lightly poached seafood or on salad greens. The mixture will separate upon standing, so whisk it before using.

4	medium-to-large firm but ripe tomatoes
1	onion, cut into ½-inch slices
1½	tablespoons olive oil
2	garlic cloves, mashed to a paste
1	tablespoon sherry vinegar or red wine vinegar
	Salt and freshly ground black pepper
4-6	tablespoons extra-virgin olive oil
2	tablespoons minced fresh herbs, such as basil, tarragon or cilantro

1. Preheat the oven to 500°F.

2. Place the tomatoes and onion slices in a small roasting pan and brush all over with the oil. Roast, turning once, for 10 to 15 minutes, or until deeply colored. Transfer to a bowl and let cool. Peel, core and chop the tomatoes.

3. In a food processor or blender, combine the tomatoes and their juices, the onion, garlic, vinegar and salt and pepper to taste and process until smooth. With the machine running, add the extra-virgin olive oil in a stream. Pour the dressing into a serving bowl and stir in the fresh herbs. Store the dressing in an airtight container in the refrigerator for up to 1 week.

Roasted Portobello Mushroom *and* Arugula Salad

Serves 4

Preparation time: 15 minutes ❖ *Cooking time: 20 minutes*

MEATY PORTOBELLO MUSHROOMS roast beautifully, without drying out or shriveling, and give off flavorful cooking juices, which are added to the salad dressing. Arugula lends its singular spicy bite. Fresh herbs are a must here. Serve as a first course.

4   large portobello mushrooms,
    each about 4 inches in diameter,
    stems removed

1½ tablespoons olive oil
    Salt and freshly ground black pepper

2   teaspoons minced fresh thyme,
    or 1 teaspoon dried, crumbled

¼   cup sherry vinegar

2   cups bite-size pieces red-leaf lettuce,
    washed and patted dry

2   cups bite-size pieces arugula,
    washed and patted dry

½   cup minced red bell pepper

¼   cup minced red onion

For the dressing

2   teaspoons Dijon mustard

½   teaspoon minced garlic

¼   cup extra-virgin olive oil

2   tablespoons minced fresh herbs,
    such as tarragon, chives, chervil
    or parsley, or a combination

1. Preheat the oven to 425°F. Lightly oil a shallow roasting pan.

2. Brush the mushroom caps with oil and season with salt and pepper to taste. Place in the roasting pan and sprinkle with the thyme. Roast, turning once, for 15 to 20 minutes, or until they are just tender and golden. Transfer the mushrooms to a cutting board.

3. Pour the vinegar into the roasting pan. Bring to a boil over high heat, scraping up the roasting juices with a wooden spoon. Remove from the heat.

4. In a large bowl, combine the lettuce, arugula, bell pepper and onion.

5. **Make the dressing:** In a small bowl, whisk together 2 tablespoons of the deglazing liquid with the mustard, garlic and salt and pepper to taste. Add the oil in a thin stream, whisking, and whisk until combined.

6. Add the dressing to the salad and toss gently. Divide the salad among 4 plates. Slice the mushrooms and arrange over the salads. Sprinkle with the fresh herbs of choice and serve.

$\mathcal{R}$oasted Pear *and* Bacon Salad *with* Blue Cheese

Serves 4

Preparation time: 15 minutes ❖ *Cooking time: 12 minutes*

HERE WE OFFER A VARIATION on the classic combination of fruit and cheese, with roasted, rather than raw, fruit. This is best served as a first course to whet the appetite, with its interplay of sweet and salty flavors. It makes a lovely luncheon starter when followed by a main-course soup.

3	Anjou, Bosc or Bartlett pears, cored and halved lengthwise	½	teaspoon sugar
			Salt and freshly ground black pepper
2	tablespoons unsalted butter, melted	2	cups bite-size pieces frisée or curly endive, washed and patted dry
4	thick slices bacon	2	cups bite-size pieces red-leaf lettuce, washed and patted dry
3	tablespoons cider vinegar		
2	tablespoons vegetable oil	6	ounces blue cheese, crumbled

1. Preheat the oven to 500°F. Butter a baking sheet.

2. Brush the pear halves with melted butter and arrange, cut side down, on the baking sheet. Roast for 10 minutes, or until heated through and just tender. Let cool for 5 minutes; cut into ½-inch-thick slices.

3. While the pears roast, roast the bacon on a rack in a small baking pan for 10 minutes, or until crisp. Drain on paper towels (reserve the drippings), let cool enough to handle and crumble.

4. Pour off all but 2 tablespoons of the bacon drippings from the pan and place the pan over medium heat. Add the vinegar and boil for 1 minute. Whisk in the oil, sugar and salt and pepper to taste. Set aside.

5. In a large bowl, combine the frisée or endive, lettuce and pears. Add the dressing and toss gently to coat. Divide the salad among 4 plates and garnish with the bacon and blue cheese. Serve warm.

Roasted Red Pepper *and* Fennel Salad

with Cannellini Beans

Serves 4
Preparation time: 10 minutes
Cooking time: 20 minutes

THIS APPEALING SALAD, which is served at room temperature, could easily serve as a main course. With a cup of soup to start and fruit to follow, it makes a light vegetarian lunch. Roasting the vegetables rather than adding them raw imparts a smoky, rich flavor.

Vary the beans as you wish. Black beans are a good alternative.

1	fennel bulb, rinsed
1	large red bell pepper, cored, seeded and cut lengthwise into 1-inch-wide strips
1	small red onion, cut into ⅓-inch-thick rounds
2	tablespoons olive oil
	Salt and freshly ground black pepper

For the dressing

2	tablespoons fresh lemon juice
2	tablespoons balsamic vinegar
1	teaspoon minced garlic
	Salt and freshly ground black pepper
¼	cup extra-virgin olive oil
2	cups canned cannellini beans or other white beans, drained and rinsed
2	tablespoons minced fresh parsley

1. Preheat the oven to 500°F.

2. Starting at the tip of the bulb, slice the fennel lengthwise into ⅓-inch-thick slices, but without cutting all the way through the core, so the slices remain attached at the bottom.

3. Place the bell pepper, fennel and onion in a shallow roasting pan, brush with the oil and season with salt and pepper to taste. Roast, turning once, for 20 minutes, or until tender and lightly golden. Transfer to a plate to cool, then cut the bell pepper and onion into dice. Separate the fennel into strips, cutting away and discarding the core.

4. **Make the dressing:** In a bowl, whisk together the lemon juice, vinegar, garlic and salt and pepper to taste. Add the oil in a thin stream, whisking, and whisk until well combined.

5. In a serving bowl, combine the vegetables with the beans. Add the dressing and toss gently to combine. Sprinkle the parsley over the top.

Roasted Tricolor Pepper Salad *with* Balsamic Vinegar, Basil *and* Pine Nuts

Serves 6
Preparation time: 2½ hours (includes roasting and marinating the peppers)
Cooking time: None

THIS SALAD IS ALMOST TOO BEAUTIFUL TO EAT—but not quite! Serve it as an antipasto, or as an accompaniment to grilled fish on parslied rice. Make sure there is plenty of crusty bread to mop up the superb dressing.

2 red bell peppers, roasted, peeled, cored, seeded, and cut into 1-inch-wide slices (see page 39)	2 tablespoons fresh lemon juice
	2 tablespoons balsamic vinegar
	2 teaspoons minced garlic
2 green bell peppers, roasted, peeled, cored, seeded and cut into 1-inch-wide slices (see page 39)	Salt and freshly ground black pepper
	3 tablespoons extra-virgin olive oil, or to taste
2 yellow or orange bell peppers, roasted, peeled, cored, seeded and cut into 1-inch-wide slices (see page 39)	3 tablespoons minced fresh basil or chives, or a combination
	3 tablespoons pine nuts, toasted (see Tip, page 177)

1. Arrange the bell peppers, alternating the colors, in a serving dish.

2. In a bowl, whisk together the lemon juice, vinegar, garlic and salt and pepper to taste. Add the oil in a thin stream, whisking, and whisk the dressing until well combined. Stir in the fresh herbs.

3. Pour the dressing over the peppers. Cover the dish with plastic wrap and let stand at room temperature for 2 hours, or chill overnight. Bring to room temperature and sprinkle the salad with the pine nuts before serving.

Roasted Leek *and* Hearts of Palm Salad

Serves 4
Preparation time: 20 minutes ❖ *Cooking time: 25 minutes*

WE LIKE TO SERVE THIS UNIQUE AND ATTRACTIVE COMBINATION as a first course. Hearts of palm, available in cans in most supermarkets, have a mild taste and texture akin to poached asparagus. The hearts of palm contrast with cooked-until-tender leeks.

4 medium-to-large leeks, white and pale green parts, well washed	2 firm but ripe tomatoes, diced
1½ tablespoons olive oil	½ cup minced scallions
Salt and freshly ground black pepper	2 tablespoons minced fresh parsley
1 cup sliced canned hearts of palm, rinsed and patted dry	2 tablespoons red wine vinegar
	¼ cup extra-virgin olive oil

1. Preheat the oven to 450°F.

2. Place the leeks in a shallow roasting pan, brush with the oil and season with salt and pepper to taste. Cover with foil and roast for 15 minutes. Remove the foil and roast for 10 minutes more, or until tender but not falling apart. Let cool.

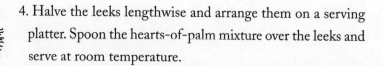

3. In a medium bowl, combine the hearts of palm, tomatoes, scallions and parsley. Add the vinegar, oil and salt and pepper to taste. Toss gently to combine.

4. Halve the leeks lengthwise and arrange them on a serving platter. Spoon the hearts-of-palm mixture over the leeks and serve at room temperature.

Roasted Herbed Potatoes Vinaigrette

Serves 4 to 6

Preparation time: 20 minutes ❖ *Cooking time: 25 minutes*

THIS POTATO SALAD is notably lighter than the old-fashioned kind with mayonnaise. The potatoes are roasted, which makes them slightly crusty on the outside and soft within—very different from boiled potatoes—and downright addictive.

2	pounds red potatoes (about 8 medium), scrubbed and cut into 1-inch pieces	½	cup diced celery
2	tablespoons olive oil	½	cup diced green bell pepper
1	tablespoon minced fresh rosemary, or 1 teaspoon dried, crumbled	2	tablespoons Dijon mustard
	Salt and freshly ground black pepper	2	tablespoons white wine vinegar
		1	teaspoon minced garlic
⅔	cup minced scallions	4-6	tablespoons extra-virgin olive oil
		2	tablespoons minced fresh parsley

1. Preheat the oven to 425°F.

2. In a shallow roasting pan, toss the potatoes with the oil. Sprinkle with the rosemary and salt and pepper to taste. Roast, turning frequently, for 25 minutes, or until golden brown and fork-tender. Let cool.

3. Put the potatoes in a serving bowl and add the scallions, celery and bell pepper.

4. In a bowl, whisk together the mustard, vinegar, garlic and salt and pepper to taste. Add the extra-virgin oil in a thin stream, whisking, and whisk until combined. Pour the dressing over the salad and toss gently to combine. Sprinkle with the parsley.

Roasted Sweet Potato Salad

Serves 4

Preparation time: 30 minutes ❖ *Cooking time: 30 minutes*

SWEET POTATOES—roasted instead of boiled—replace ordinary potatoes here, and the salad is dressed with a refreshing citrusy vinaigrette. This salad is substantial enough for a light lunch, with fruit for dessert. Or serve as a first course, as a prelude to Loin of Pork Roasted with Honey and Mustard (page 156).

1 pound sweet potatoes (about 2 medium), peeled and cut into 1-inch pieces	3 tablespoons raspberry vinegar
¼ cup olive oil	1 teaspoon minced garlic
Salt and freshly ground black pepper	1 teaspoon grated orange zest
2 tablespoons unsalted butter, softened	¼ cup minced shallots (2 large)
2 teaspoons minced fresh ginger	2 cups mixed baby greens (mesclun)
6 tablespoons fresh orange juice	4 thick slices bacon
1 tablespoon fresh lemon juice	2 tablespoons snipped fresh chives or scallion tops

1. Preheat the oven to 450°F.

2. In a roasting pan, toss the potatoes with 2 tablespoons of the oil and salt and pepper to taste. Roast the potatoes on the bottom rack of the oven, turning them once, for 20 minutes. Add the butter, ginger, 4 tablespoons of the orange juice, the lemon juice and salt and pepper to taste; toss to coat. Move the pan to the middle of the oven and roast, basting occasionally with the pan juices, for 10 minutes more, or until tender when tested with a fork.

3. Meanwhile, in a large skillet, cook the bacon over medium heat until crisp. Drain on paper towels, cut into 1-inch pieces and set aside.

4. In a bowl, whisk together the remaining 2 tablespoons orange juice, the vinegar, garlic, orange zest and salt and pepper to taste. Add the remaining 2 tablespoons oil in a thin stream, whisking, and whisk until the dressing is combined.

5. While the potatoes are still warm, put them in a bowl and add the shallots and all but 2 tablespoons of the dressing; toss gently.

6. In another bowl, toss the greens with the reserved 2 tablespoons dressing. Divide them among 4 salad plates. Top the greens with the potato salad and garnish with the bacon and chives or scallions.

Roasted Stuffed Chicken Breast Salad

Serves 4
Preparation time: 35 minutes (includes making the dressing)
Cooking time: 25 minutes

THIS CHICKEN SALAD, tossed with a roasted tomato and onion dressing, is remarkably sophisticated, considering how easy it is to make. The ingredients—sun-dried tomatoes, goat cheese, arugula, avocado—interact beautifully with roasted chicken.

Serve this for a light lunch or a summer supper. Raspberries garnished with candied orange peel and a touch of Grand Marnier would make a fitting dessert.

4   6-ounce boneless chicken
      breast halves with skin
      Salt and freshly ground black pepper
6   ounces fresh goat cheese, such
      as Montrachet or Bucheron
      (not the type coated with ash)
¼   cup drained, minced oil-packed
      sun-dried tomatoes
3   tablespoons freshly grated Parmesan
3   tablespoons minced scallion
1   garlic clove, minced

2   tablespoons olive oil
2   cups arugula leaves, washed
      and patted dry
3   cups bite-size pieces leaf lettuce,
      washed and patted dry
½   cup sliced red onion
1   California (Hass) avocado,
      peeled, pitted and cubed

Roasted Tomato and Onion Dressing
   (page 205)

1. Preheat the oven to 500°F.

2. With the point of a sharp knife, cut a slit in the thick portion of each of the chicken breasts to create a pocket and season with salt and pepper.

3. In a small bowl, mash the goat cheese, sun-dried tomatoes, Parmesan, scallion, garlic and salt and pepper to taste. Stuff the mixture into the pockets in the chicken breasts, gently pressing the edges of the pockets closed. If necessary, secure with toothpicks. Brush the chicken with the oil, season with salt and pepper to taste, place in a roasting pan and roast for 8 to 10 minutes, or until the juices run clear. Remove to a plate and let rest, covered, for 5 minutes.

4. In a large bowl, combine the arugula, lettuce, onion and avocado. Add enough of the dressing to coat the vegetables and toss well. Divide the mixture among 4 serving plates.

5. Slice each chicken breast on the diagonal and arrange the slices on top of the greens. Drizzle with the remaining dressing and serve.

Peppered Tuna Salad Niçoise

Serves 4
Preparation time: 40 minutes (includes chilling the tuna)
Cooking time: 7 to 11 minutes

POTATOES, GREEN BEANS, TOMATOES, EGGS AND OLIVES—all the classic components of a Niçoise salad are here. But for the usual canned tuna, we've substituted fresh tuna steaks, coated with pepper and quick-roasted to rare—our preference. If longer-cooked tuna is more appealing to you, we have also included the roasting time for that.

With the vegetables and eggs prepared ahead of time, you can serve these salads in a mere 20 minutes—healthy, delicious, fast food!

4   8-ounce tuna steaks, cut 1 inch thick
1   tablespoon cracked black pepper
2   cups cubed red potatoes
2   cups green beans, cut into
      1½-inch lengths
    Salt
2   tablespoons olive oil
1   cup red cherry tomatoes, halved
1   cup yellow cherry tomatoes, halved

For the dressing
1   tablespoon Dijon mustard
1   tablespoon balsamic vinegar
2   tablespoons fresh lemon juice

1   garlic clove, mashed to a paste
    Salt and freshly ground black pepper
½   cup olive oil, or to taste
2   tablespoons snipped fresh dill or chives
      or minced fresh basil or parsley

    Boston or other soft-leaf lettuce,
      washed and patted dry,
      for lining the plates
2   hard-cooked eggs, peeled
      and cut into quarters
12 black olives, such as Niçoise
      or kalamata

1. Pat the tuna steaks dry and gently press the cracked pepper onto all sides. Cover and refrigerate for 30 minutes.

2. In a medium saucepan, combine the potatoes with enough water to cover by 2 inches. Bring to a boil over medium-high heat and simmer for 12 to 15 minutes, or until the potatoes are just tender. Drain and let cool.

3. Place the beans in a saucepan of boiling, salted water, and cook for 5 minutes, or until just tender. Drain and refresh under cold water. Pat dry and set aside.

4. Preheat the oven to 500°F.

5. Season the tuna with salt and brush both sides with the oil. Place on a baking sheet and roast for 7 minutes for rare, 8 to 9 minutes for medium-rare or 10 to 11 minutes for medium.

6. Meanwhile, combine the potatoes, green beans and tomatoes in a large bowl.

7. **Make the dressing:** In a small bowl, whisk together the mustard, vinegar, lemon juice, garlic and salt and pepper to taste. Add the oil in a thin stream, whisking, and whisk until well combined. Whisk in the herbs.

8. Add enough dressing to the vegetables to coat them well. Line 4 serving plates with the lettuce leaves, arrange the vegetables over the lettuce and top with the tuna. Garnish with the eggs and olives and drizzle with the remaining dressing.

Chapter VIII

Desserts

Something wonderful happens to the sugars in fruits when they are subjected to high heat. As their juice begins to evaporate, their natural sugars brown and take on complex overtones. The texture of roasted fruit changes, too, becoming softer and more yielding. This chapter includes a dozen roasted fruit desserts, ranging from apples and figs to peaches and pears.

Fruit that will be roasted must be at just the right stage of ripeness "Firm but ripe" says it all. The pear, peach, plum or nectarine in question should have a sweet identifiable aroma and just give when gently squeezed. Apples should be crisp-hard. For fresh pineapple, a sweet smell is the most foolproof indication of ripeness; it should yield slightly when pressed. If you can detect no softness in the fruit you are considering, keep looking. Not even roasting can alter the texture of rock-hard fruit.

Some of the recipes that follow are remarkable for their simplicity. Roasted Bananas with Caramel Sauce (page 230) takes only 10 minutes to cook and 15 minutes to prepare. Roasted Bing Cherries (page 229) is easier still, requiring a mere four ingredients.

Other recipes echo time-honored combinations, like Roasted Bread with Pears and Gorgonzola (page 240). There are also foolproof alternatives to the longer-cooking favorites like crisps and cobblers, namely Peach Bruschetta (page 241) and Raspberry Croûtes (page 242).

A good number of the recipes can roast while you're at the table enjoying dinner, making them additionally sweet rewards.

Desserts

$\mathcal{R}$oasted Spiced Apples

Serves 4

Preparation time: 10 minutes ❖ *Cooking time: 55 minutes*

YOU NEED ONLY 10 MINUTES to prepare this old-fashioned dessert for roasting, and then the oven does the work as a delicious aroma fills the house.

Although these are usually served for dessert, they are also good at breakfast, with a little heavy cream. Follow them with sausages and homemade biscuits.

4 large baking apples, such as Rome Beauty or McIntosh	Pinch of ground cloves
⅓ cup chopped walnuts	1 cup apple cider
⅓ cup firmly packed light brown sugar	⅓ cup honey
3 tablespoons unsalted butter, softened	2 tablespoons fresh lemon juice
½ teaspoon ground cinnamon	Whipped cream or vanilla ice cream,
¼ teaspoon freshly grated nutmeg	for serving

1. Preheat the oven to 400°F. Core the apples to within ½ inch of the base, leaving the bottoms intact. Peel the top third of each apple.

2. In a small bowl, combine the walnuts, brown sugar, butter, cinnamon, nutmeg and cloves. Fill the apples with the walnut mixture, then fit the apples snugly into a flameproof baking dish.

3. In a separate small bowl, combine the cider, honey and lemon juice. Pour the cider mixture around the apples, then roast, basting frequently, for 45 to 50 minutes, or until tender. Arrange in a serving dish, reserving the pan juices.

4. Over high heat, reduce the cooking liquid until syrupy, about 5 minutes. Spoon the syrup over the apples and serve hot, warm or at room temperature with whipped cream or ice cream.

Roasted Pineapple

Serves 4

Preparation time: 15 minutes ❖ *Cooking time: 17 minutes*

YOU CAN ROAST THESE PINEAPPLE SLICES in the time it takes to brew a pot of coffee. To get the requisite eight slices, look for a pineapple that weighs about one and a half pounds. The Hawaiian-grown ones are the sweetest. A sweet aroma is a good indication of ripeness.

Garnish the warm pineapple with partially thawed frozen raspberries or sliced strawberries with a bit of their syrup. Garnish with a fresh mint leaf, and you have an elegant, refreshing finale, with no fat. Dessert doesn't get much easier than this.

8	slices peeled fresh pineapple, about ½ inch thick	½	teaspoon grated lemon zest
		1-2	tablespoons fresh lemon juice
⅓	cup honey, or more to taste	1	tablespoon dark rum (optional)

1. Preheat the oven to 425°F. Butter a shallow 9-x-12-inch flameproof baking dish.

2. Arrange the pineapple slices in a single layer in the dish. In a small bowl, combine the honey, lemon zest and juice and the rum, if using. Pour the mixture over the pineapple. Roast for 10 to 15 minutes, or until heated through.

3. Preheat the broiler. Place the dish under the broiler and broil for 1 to 2 minutes, or until the slices are well glazed; watch carefully. Serve hot.

Roasted Bing Cherries

Serves 4

Preparation time: 15 minutes ❖ *Cooking time: 15 minutes*

EATING CHERRIES OUT OF HAND IS GREAT, but it's not the only way to enjoy them. See if this unexpected preparation doesn't tempt you with its simplicity. The flavor of a roasted cherry is similar to that of a dried cherry—sweet and concentrated—but its texture is softer. Pitting the cherries goes much faster with a cherry pitter, available in most kitchenware stores.

Serve plain, as a sauce for slightly softened ice cream or over toasted pound cake. Roasted cherry shortcakes, made with homemade baking powder biscuits and whipped cream, would be wonderful too.

1 **pound Bing cherries, pitted**	3 **tablespoons unsalted butter**
⅓ **cup sugar, or more to taste**	⅓ **cup kirsch**

1. Preheat the oven to 400°F. Butter a large shallow baking pan.

2. Spread the cherries in a single layer in the pan, sprinkle with the sugar and dot with the butter. Roast for 15 minutes.

3. Remove the pan from the oven, add the kirsch and bring to a boil, scraping the bottom of the pan with a spoon. Transfer the cherries and cooking liquid to a serving bowl and let cool. Serve at room temperature.

Roasted Bananas *with* Caramel Sauce

Serves 4
Preparation time: 10 minutes (includes toasting the nuts)
Cooking time: 20 minutes

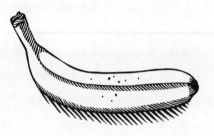

NOT MANY DESSERTS CALL FOR COOKED BANANAS—the exception being the great New Orleans favorite, bananas Foster, which are sautéed in a mixture of butter, brown sugar, cinnamon and banana liqueur, then topped with vanilla ice cream. For this takeoff on that dish, we decided to try roasted, as opposed to sautéed, bananas. Topped with caramel sauce and a few nuts, they are ambrosial.

Start with firm bananas. To hasten the ripening of green bananas, put them in a plastic bag with another ethylene-gas-producing fruit, like an apple. Seal the bag. The bananas will soften within a day or two.

For the caramel sauce
1   cup sugar
1   cup heavy cream
1-2 tablespoons dark rum

4 firm but ripe bananas
¼ cup chopped macadamia nuts,
    toasted (see Tip)

1. Preheat the oven to 450°F. Butter a gratin dish large enough to hold the bananas in a single layer.

2. **Make the caramel sauce:** In a heavy saucepan, combine the sugar with ⅓ cup water and bring to a boil over high heat, stirring. Continue to boil, brushing down the sides of the pan occasionally with a brush dipped in cold water, until the syrup is golden brown, about 5 minutes. Remove from the heat and slowly stir in the cream until combined; be careful, the mixture will bubble up. Return the pan to low heat and add the rum, stirring.

3. Arrange the bananas in the gratin dish, pour the sauce over them and turn to coat. Roast, turning occasionally, for 6 to 10 minutes, or until heated through. Transfer the bananas and sauce to a serving dish and sprinkle the nuts over the top.

❖ **To toast macadamia nuts, place in a small, dry skillet over medium heat and toast, stirring occasionally, for 2 to 3 minutes, or until golden brown. Remove from the skillet and let cool.**

*R*oasted Prune Plums *with* Almond Topping

Serves 6 to 8

Preparation time: 20 minutes ❖ *Cooking time: 40 minutes*

THIS SIMPLE, COMFORTING FRUIT CRISP is updated by the addition of slivered almonds. You'll need prune plums for it. They are usually available in late summer. Don't try to substitute red Santa Rosas or Friars: Neither variety can withstand the high heat, and both are too juicy for the topping. Serve with softened vanilla ice cream or heavy cream. The dish is good for brunch too.

2 pounds prune plums, halved, pitted and sliced	**For the almond topping**
⅓ cup firmly packed light brown sugar	⅔ cup flour
¼ cup sugar	¾ cup slivered or sliced blanched almonds
½ teaspoon ground cinnamon	¼ cup firmly packed light brown sugar
1 tablespoon flour	¼ cup sugar
1 tablespoon fresh lemon juice	½ teaspoon ground cinnamon
2 tablespoons cold unsalted butter, cut into bits	Pinch of salt
	6 tablespoons (¾ stick) cold unsalted butter, cut into bits

1. Preheat the oven to 425°F. Butter a shallow 10-inch round baking dish, 2 inches deep.

2. In a large bowl, combine the plums, brown sugar, sugar, cinnamon, flour and lemon juice and toss. Spread in the baking dish and dot with the butter. Roast, stirring occasionally, for 15 to 20 minutes, or until the plums begin to give off their juices.

3. **Meanwhile, make the almond topping:** In a medium bowl, combine the flour, nuts, sugars, cinnamon and salt. Cut the butter into the dry ingredients, using a pastry blender or 2 forks, until the mixture resembles coarse meal.

4. Sprinkle the topping over the partially baked plums. Roast the plums for 20 minutes longer, or until just tender. Serve warm.

ROASTED GINGERED NECTARINES WITH PECAN TOPPING

Serves 6 to 8

Preparation time: 20 minutes ❖ *Cooking time: 40 minutes*

THIS DISH IS DELICIOUS for breakfast or brunch as well as for dessert. If nectarines aren't at their best, substitute peeled peaches. To prepare and roast, follow the directions for Roasted Prune Plums with Almond Topping (page 232), adding the crystallized ginger to the fruit mixture.

6 medium-to-large nectarines,
   peeled, pitted and sliced

⅓ cup firmly packed light brown sugar

1 tablespoon flour

3 tablespoons minced crystallized ginger

1 teaspoon grated lemon zest

1 tablespoon fresh lemon juice

2 tablespoons cold unsalted butter,
   cut into bits

For the pecan topping

⅔ cup flour

1 cup chopped pecans, toasted
   (see Tip, page 139)

¼ cup firmly packed light brown sugar

¼ cup sugar

¼ teaspoon freshly grated nutmeg

   Pinch of salt

6 tablespoons (¾ stick) cold unsalted
   butter, cut into bits

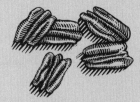

Roasted Figs *with* Mascarpone

Serves 4

Preparation time: 10 minutes (includes toasting the nuts) ❖ *Cooking time: 15 minutes*

ROASTED AND GARNISHED WITH MASCARPONE, the rich Italian cow's-milk cheese, fresh figs are unimaginably decadent. Look for mascarpone in gourmet markets, Italian food stores or well-stocked supermarkets. If you can't find it, substitute ricotta or crème fraîche.

12 firm but ripe figs, such as Calimyrna, halved	1 cup ruby port
2-3 tablespoons sugar	½ cup mascarpone (or ricotta or crème fraîche, sweetened with sugar to taste)
½ teaspoon ground cinnamon	¼ cup sliced blanched almonds, toasted
3 tablespoons unsalted butter	(see Tip), for garnish (optional)

1. Preheat the oven to 450°F. Butter a shallow flameproof baking dish large enough to hold the figs in a single layer.

2. Arrange the figs, cut side up, in the baking dish, sprinkle with the sugar and cinnamon and dot with the butter. Roast for 10 to 15 minutes, or until heated through. Transfer the figs to a platter. Place the baking dish over high heat, add the port and bring to a boil, boiling for 1 minute, scraping the bottom of the baking dish. Pour the liquid over the figs and cool to room temperature.

3. To serve, divide the figs with their liquid among 4 goblets, top with the mascarpone, ricotta or crème fraîche and sprinkle with the almonds, if desired.

❖ To toast almonds, place in a small, dry skillet over medium heat and toast, stirring occasionally, for about 3 minutes, or until golden brown. Remove from the skillet and let cool.

$\mathcal{R}$oasted Peaches *with* Amaretti

Serves 4

Preparation time: 20 minutes ❖ *Cooking time: 30 minutes*

THIS WARM DESSERT is perfect for the first cool days of late summer, when peaches are still plentiful but long hours of baking are not something you are eager to begin quite yet. Try this with the best peaches of all—the white ones—and if you are feeling really indulgent, serve with a scoop of homemade vanilla or peach ice cream.

⅔ cup sugar

½ cup heavy cream

¼ teaspoon pure vanilla extract

1 tablespoon brandy

4 large, ripe peaches, peeled, halved and pitted

½ cup crushed amaretti (imported Italian macaroon cookies)

1. Preheat the oven to 425°F. Butter a flameproof baking dish large enough to hold the peaches in a single layer.

2. In a medium saucepan, combine the sugar with ¼ cup water and bring to a boil over high heat, stirring until the sugar is dissolved. Continue to boil, brushing down the sides of the pan occasionally with a brush dipped in cold water, until the syrup is golden brown, 3 to 5 minutes. Remove from the heat and slowly stir in the cream until combined; be careful, the mixture will bubble up. Return the pan to low heat and stir in the vanilla and brandy.

3. Arrange the peaches, cut side down, in the baking dish and pour the sauce over them. Roast, basting frequently with the pan juices, for 10 minutes. Turn the peaches cut sides up and roast, basting frequently, for 10 minutes more, or until tender.

4. Preheat the broiler. Place the baking dish under the broiler and broil for 1 to 2 minutes, or until glazed; watch carefully.

5. To serve, put the peaches in a serving dish, nap them with the caramel sauce and sprinkle the amaretti over the top.

Roasted Pears *with*

Almond-Flavored Custard Sauce

Serves 4

Preparation time: 10 minutes ❖ *Cooking time: 1 hour*

PEARS AND ALMONDS make a fragrant combination. This dessert, a welcome change from the usual poached pears, is easy to make but sophisticated, in large part because of its soothing sauce. To maximize the flavors, serve warm.

4	firm but ripe Bosc pears, peeled, halved lengthwise and cored
2	tablespoons fresh lemon juice
2	tablespoons unsalted butter
¼	cup firmly packed light brown sugar
½	teaspoon grated lemon zest
½	teaspoon ground cinnamon
¼	teaspoon freshly grated nutmeg
	Pinch of ground cloves

For the custard sauce

2	large egg yolks
1	large egg
¼	cup sugar
1	cup half-and-half, heated until small bubbles appear
½	teaspoon pure vanilla extract
¼	teaspoon almond extract
1	tablespoon almond-flavored liqueur (optional)

Sliced blanched almonds, toasted (see page 235), for garnish

1. Preheat the oven to 400°F. Butter a gratin dish large enough to hold the pears in a single layer.

2. Sprinkle the pears with 1 tablespoon of the lemon juice.

3. In a small saucepan, melt the butter over medium-low heat. Add the remaining 1 tablespoon lemon juice, the brown sugar, lemon zest, cinnamon, nutmeg and cloves, and cook, stirring, until smooth. Arrange the pears, cut side down, in the gratin dish, spoon the brown sugar mixture over them. Roast, basting frequently with the pan juices, for 50 minutes, or until tender.

4. **Meanwhile, make the custard sauce:** In a medium bowl, whisk together the egg yolks, egg and sugar. Whisk in the half-and-half and transfer the mixture to a heavy saucepan. Cook over medium-low heat, stirring, until the custard is thickened slightly and coats the back of a spoon, about 10 minutes. Do not let it boil. Remove from the heat and stir in the vanilla and almond extracts and the liqueur, if using.

5. Arrange the pears in a shallow serving dish, spoon the custard sauce over them and sprinkle with the toasted almonds.

Roasted Bread *with* Pears *and* Gorgonzola

Serves 4
Preparation time: 10 minutes ❖ Cooking time: 21 minutes

ROASTING PEARS UNDER A SUGARY TOPPING brings out the best in them, softening them slightly and enhancing their flavor. Paired with a strong cheese like Gorgonzola, these pear croûtes make a savory finale to a robust meal, the kind you would serve in fall or winter, when the best pears are available.

4 thick slices day-old country bread	2 firm but ripe pears, such as Bosc,
4 tablespoons (½ stick) unsalted butter,	Bartlett or Anjou, peeled, cored
softened	and sliced ½ inch thick
	Sugar
	4-6 ounces Gorgonzola cheese, crumbled

1. Preheat the oven to 450°F.

2. Spread each bread slice with 1 tablespoon of the butter, top with the pear slices and sprinkle with sugar to taste. Arrange on a baking sheet and roast for 20 minutes, or until the pears are tender.

3. Preheat the broiler. Place the baking sheet under the broiler and broil until the pears are glazed, about 1 minute. Transfer the croûtes to dessert plates and sprinkle with the Gorgonzola. Serve immediately.

Peach Bruschetta

Serves 4

Preparation time: 10 minutes ❖ *Cooking time: 21 minutes*

WHEN YOU ARE ROASTING SLICED FRUIT on bread at 450°F, you can be sure of one thing: Dessert will be on the table fast. These bruschetta, which should be made with the best of summertime fruits, whether peaches, plums or nectarines, are as comforting as crisps and crumbles but much quicker to prepare.

4 ½-inch-thick slices day-old firm bread	¼ cup sugar or honey, or to taste
2 tablespoons unsalted butter, softened	Ground cinnamon or freshly
4 medium peaches, nectarines or plums, peeled, pitted and cut into ¼-inch-thick slices	grated nutmeg

1. Preheat the oven to 450°F.

2. Spread each bread slice with ½ tablespoon of the butter and top with the fruit and sugar or honey. Sprinkle with cinnamon or nutmeg to taste. Carefully transfer to a baking sheet and roast for 20 minutes.

3. Preheat the broiler. Place the baking sheet under the broiler and broil until the fruit is nicely glazed, about 1 minute. Serve at once.

Raspberry Croûtes

Serves 4

Preparation time: 5 minutes ❖ *Cooking time: 20 minutes*

THESE DESSERT CROÛTES could just as easily be served for breakfast or as an elegant snack. Combine the berries with a stone fruit, like diced peaches or nectarines, if desired. You can substitute firm-textured pound cake for the baguette.

4	½-inch-thick diagonally cut slices day-old baguette	½	pint raspberries
2	tablespoons unsalted butter, softened	3-4	teaspoons sugar

1. Preheat the oven to 450°F.

2. Spread each bread slice with ½ tablespoon of the butter and top with the raspberries. Sprinkle with the sugar.

3. Transfer to a baking sheet and roast for 15 to 20 minutes, or until heated through. Serve at once.

Roasted Brioche *and* Chocolate Sandwiches

Serves 4
Preparation time: 5 minutes ❖ *Cooking time: 10 minutes*

THE FRENCH HAVE LONG KNOWN how marvelous melted chocolate can be when enclosed in layers of warm, flaky pastry. However, making *pains au chocolat* is a task for the experienced baker, and finding good ones in American bakeries is not easy. The next best thing? An improvisation that gives some of the effect and a lot of the pleasure. Around the holidays, try substituting leftover panettone or stollen for the bread. These make fast snacks after school for kids, or serve with a cup of fresh-brewed coffee or tea for grown-ups.

4   ½-inch-thick slices brioche,
      challah or similar bread
1   3½-to-4-ounce bar good-quality
      bittersweet chocolate,
      ¼ inch thick, halved

2   tablespoons unsalted butter, softened
      Sifted confectioners' sugar, for garnish
      Whole unhulled strawberries,
         for serving (optional)

1. Preheat the oven to 450°F.

2. Top 2 slices of the bread with the chocolate, leaving a ½-inch border. Top with the remaining bread. Spread both sides of the sandwiches with the butter and place on a baking sheet. Roast for 5 minutes on each side, or until the chocolate is melted and the bread is golden brown.

3. Transfer the sandwiches to a cutting board and let cool for 5 minutes. Halve the sandwiches on the diagonal and dust with confectioners' sugar. Arrange on serving plates and garnish with strawberries, if desired.

Index

About the Authors

GEORGIA CHAN DOWNARD AND EVIE RIGHTER BEGAN COLLABORATING as editors at *Gourmet* magazine. Georgia Downard is culinary director of Television Food Network. She is author of *The Big Broccoli Book* (Random House) and co-author of *365 Ways to Cook Soups and Stews* (HarperCollins). Evie Righter is a cookbook editor and former scriptwriter for Television Food Network. Her books include *The Best of France*, *The Best of Italy* and *The Best of China* (HarperCollins).